It Just Hasn't
Happened Yet!

bogus, ridiculous, absurd
explanations as to
why you're still single
and how to deal with them

plus a few silly things we
do to ourselves

Karin Anderson, Ph.D.

Praise for
It Just Hasn't Happened Yet

"*It Just Hasn't Happened Yet* is a Must Read. Written as a conversation between girl friends, mothers and daughters, young (and not so young) women and a guy friend or some experts, the book demolishes all the advice in most self help books for singles, while illustrating all the negative social pressures on single women. Dr. Anderson's perspective challenges single women, and all those around them, to change their viewpoint. It's fun and informative."

— Dr. Kay Trimberger, sociologist and
author, *The New Single Woman*

"At last! A book that acknowledges that, while marriage can be a lovely thing, it need not be the holy grail for single women. Reading *It Just Hasn't Happened Yet* is like spending time with a wise, funny, loving girlfriend who genuinely has your best interest at heart."

— Cary Barbor, writer for *Match.com* and former
health editor, *More* Magazine

"Funny, breezy, and oh-so-practical—a sorely-needed sanity check in a relationship-crazed world."

— Leslie Talbot, author of *Singular Existence:
Because It's Better to Be Alone
Than to Wish You Were!*

"It's a clearly thought out book, with a lot of great advice on how we may not have found the one yet, but that's not a reason to settle for whoever comes along next. . . Karin's insight into the world of why people ask us these at times rude and embarrassing questions is truly worth a read. She's light-hearted and funny, yet full of worthwhile information."

— Amanda Perkins, Urban Bachelorette at *www.urbanbachelorette.com*

"What sets apart Karin Anderson's new book. . . is a glorious lack of blame, accompanied by a daring refusal to fix anyone's problems. . . Anderson. . . strenuously resists the idea that single women are by definition doing 'something wrong,' and in fact advocates a healthy acceptance of whatever relationship status a woman happens to find herself in."

— Paula Carino at *www.breakupgirl.net*

To all my single girls:
You're so money
and you don't even know it!

Table of Contents

Part 1

bogus, ridiculous, absurd explanations as to why you're
still single and how to deal with them

It Just Hasn't Happened Yet and. . .

Part 2

a few silly things we do to ourselves

It Just Hasn't Happened Yet so. . .

Introduction

Everyone tells me I'm too picky. I used to get defensive, but now I'm wondering if they're right. Maybe all the good ones have been snatched up.

— Julie, 31

I'm such a sucker for bad boys who need fixing and losers who want a woman to take care of them. I just wish for once I could find myself attracted to a nice guy!

— Gina, 37

I had a big crush on my psych prof in college and he explained that I have major daddy issues. It's like I want my boyfriends to meet needs my deadbeat dad never met.

— Ashley, 24

We've got it all figured out, don't we? Thanks to a healthy diet of *Cosmo* quizzes and *Dr. Phil* episodes, we know exactly why we're still

5

single. Most of us have analyzed this "problem" *ad nauseam* and picked our pet pathology—daddy issues, bad boys, or emotional baggage. Any pop-psych cliché will do.

Determined to fix our flawed and failing love-lives, we search for answers, figuring if we could just knock it off—stop being so neurotic and get a little more normal—we'd meet "The One". Or so we think.

At least, that's what I thought. Understand, I'm speaking from *way* too much experience. At 40, I've had plenty of years to scrutinize my dating history. And in efforts to sort it all out, I've done what we all do—dissected my "issues" over brunch with the girls and begged gay friends to divulge the mysteries of the male mind: "Come on, I know you think I'm fabulous, but what if you were straight? What would you think of me *then*?" I've vowed to play by the man-snagging rules and change any husband-repelling habits. I've sworn to transform and reform and convert and rework and do whatever it takes to bring Mr. Right my way. I've been that insecure, self-deprecating single girl and so have most of my smart, sophisticated, savvy single friends.

And then, after years of being that girl, I got tired of being that girl. So I stopped. And started writing this book.

Author's Note

Even though all the scenes in this book actually occurred and are based on real events, the names, ages, and other identifying information regarding the individuals involved have been changed.

Key

Every chapter consists of the same format, so here's a key to help you follow along:

PSYCH 101:

In this section I analyze the chapter's theme and explain it a bit so we can (maybe) not be so irritated when it happens. And in Part 2 of the book, I break down why we sometimes do silly things to ourselves. Don't worry, I call it Psych 101, but it's not like a boring college lecture—promise!

It just hasn't happened yet:

After objectively examining the situation, I get back to the parts that are nevertheless annoying and help us figure out ways to deal with them.

Key

Ditto:

Here's where someone else speaks to the issue at
hand. She may be a writer, researcher, or a fellow
single woman putting up with the same stuff we
are. It sure helps to know we're not alone.

Girl Talk:

In this section I receive a letter related to the
chapter's topic. Sometimes the writer agrees with
me, sometimes she doesn't, but we hash it out
woman-to-woman.

The Awful Truth:

The scripts presented in this segment depict
(unfortunately) a "slice of life". Each one describes
an actual scenario encountered by a single woman.
And, as the title suggests, it ain't pretty.

Guy Talk:

Well, I figured we should get the male perspective, right? This book talks a lot about guys, so it seemed prudent to let one have the floor from time to time.

Shout Out:

My final words of encouragement to you.

Part 1

It Just Hasn't Happened Yet!

bogus, ridiculous, absurd
explanations as to
why you're still single
and how to deal with them

chapter 1

It Just Hasn't Happened Yet and It's Not Your Fault!
so stop beating yourself up!

I'm totally fed up hearing comments implying there's something wrong with me just because I don't have a man—statements like that are hurtful! It's really sad that people see being single as meaning there's something wrong with you, and I'm so over all the lame advice about how to meet someone!

—Allison, 26

It's not your fault you're still single. Yes, you read that correctly. Read it again if you need to. Let it sink in. You haven't done *anything* wrong and you don't need to change *anything* about yourself in order to find "The One".

Seriously. I know some of you don't believe me and it may take the entire book for you to internalize this, but it's not your fault you haven't met him. It just hasn't happened yet.

Not that I'm surprised by your resistance. I know what I'm up against. You probably aren't hearing this sort of perspective anywhere else. In fact, if you've been single for any length of time, you've likely endured plenty of allegations bearing the exact opposite sentiment. Friends ask about your relationships in a sleuth-like manner, searching for clues as to where you're screwing up: "So, what exactly happened with Kevin? I thought this one was finally working out. . ." Sometimes their teasing subtly veils accusations: "Honey, what's going on? You always chase the good ones away!" or "Have you ever thought about getting a little therapy to figure this stuff out?" Then again, the occasional aunt, brother, or coworker blatantly accuses, "You're way too _____! No wonder you're still single!"

Even if you're lucky enough to have sensitive friends and strong family support you still get hit by the antagonistic portrayals of single women so firmly embedded in our mass media and pop culture. Consider chick flicks depicting quirky, lovelorn women who, after Pygmalion-esque metamorphoses, emerge "fixed" and finally suitable for marriage. Or flip through the latest issue of any number of women's magazines. Notice the attention devoted to helping single women identify "Dating Don'ts" and relationship *faux pas*—articles such as "Stop Scaring Him Off: The Real Reason He Didn't Call" or "Silly Girl Stuff That Guys Hate" or "Needy Moves You Must Nix: Nine Ways Women Come Off as Too Dependent".

By our late 20s, if not sooner, we get the picture—something's drastically wrong with us or else we'd have already snagged ourselves a man. Caving under the onslaught of messages from chick flicks, fashion mags, and our Aunt Barbara, we internalize the undesirable truth. "Face it," we tell ourselves, "the common denominator in all my failed relationships is *me*. I'm doing something wrong. It's my fault I'm single."

PSYCH 101: WHY WE DO IT

Why do we blame ourselves? Why take the brunt of it? Why believe it's entirely our fault we're still single? Actually, there's a bit of twisted logic at work here. We may be single, but we're not stupid.

The method to this masochistic madness? By blaming ourselves, we gain a measure of control. That's right. Rather than revealing some inveterate self-loathing, the "blame game" merely exposes a need for control. *Thanks*, you're saying. *Now you're calling us all control freaks.*

Well, maybe not freaks, but we do like our control. It's only natural. Think about it. In today's world, women have more command over more areas of our lives than ever before. We take charge of our education, strategically maneuver our career, and independently manage our finances. When things go wrong in one of these areas, we know who the culprit is—us! We've dropped the ball or taken a wrong turn. So when something's amok in our love life (like, we don't have one), we come to the same conclusion: we must have screwed it up.

In targeting ourselves, we begin a nasty regimen of self-blame that, although a bit painful at first, ultimately produces hope. *Wait,* you're saying, *blame leads to hope? Exactly how does that work?* Simple. It puts the control in our hands, right where we like it. We tell ourselves, *If I'm the one ruining my love life, then I'm the one who can fix it. All I have to do is go to Barnes & Noble, find the right book, and become an entirely different person! Then I'll find true love and lasting happiness. Problem solved!*

I mean, consider the alternative. If it's not our fault we're single, who gets the blame? Karma? Fate? God? The Universe? These forces lie well beyond our jurisdiction. If they're at fault, there's nothing we can do about it. But if it's our misstep, we can correct it.

So, while I hate hearing my smart, sexy, cream-of-the-crop, A-list, single friends berate themselves for tragic flaws, tacky habits, and troublesome neuroses, I get it. I get why they adopt this diffident demeanor and denounce their defects. The self-inflicted sucker punches are well worth it; they allow us to feel in control.

It just hasn't happened yet

But just because I get it doesn't mean I support it. It's tough enough that our love lives haven't played out as planned, yet we go and exacerbate the situation by accusing ourselves of ruining our chances for romance. More pain!

And to control the situation we try to correct the "problem" by taking charge as we would at the office. We conduct a needs-based assessment, identify weaknesses, and submit a detailed analysis with suggestions for revision—all in anticipation of increased outcomes.

Except in this case, the *needs-based assessment* is conducted on us. The *weaknesses identified* target our core, unique qualities. *Suggestions for revision* may or may not be realistic. *Increased outcomes?* After ripping our egos to shreds, I don't think so.

How cruel! Guilty of destroying our love lives we scrutinize ourselves, pin-pointing some random personality trait, physical imperfection, or emotional idiosyncrasy that *must* go in order for us to prove acceptable to the opposite sex? Talk about kicking a girl when she's down.

And the worst part? We're not controlling a darn thing. We're just beating ourselves up. This exercise in masochism doesn't bring us any closer to love and happiness. Give me a break! All we've done is lowered our self-esteem in efforts to correct a situation that, actually, we can't do anything about anyway. Nice.

Ditto

Take heart, it's nothing personal. Even the most beautiful, sophisticated, and talented single women are suspect—women like *über* successful Sheryl Crow who recounts this exchange when she ran into another well-known personality and heard, "I was just thinking about you the other day! I was thinking she's such a great girl, why doesn't she get married and have kids?"

Crow's reaction? "I felt like the breath rushed out of my body. I couldn't believe somebody was actually voicing what most of America probably thinks of me. I know it seems odd to people—if you're not married by a certain age you're either gay, asexual, or a freak who can't get along with anybody."

Girl Talk

Karin,

So, you're trying to tell me it's not my fault I'm single and I love that—I'm totally down with the *message. All this grrrrl power stuff is really cute and all, but in my case, I <u>am</u> the problem. It's my fault I'm single—totally and completely.*

To be honest, I'm kind of a freak when it comes to relationships. I always end up destroying them. Obviously I don't mean to; it's just that when I'm dating someone and getting to know him, I want to be around him all the time. I get totally caught up in it. But it always backfires because my boyfriends tell me I'm clingy and insecure—which I am! Of course this usually pushes them away. Guys hate the whole "needy" thing. So I end up getting dumped. See, I told you, it <u>is</u> my fault! I can admit it, but I can't seem to change it!

Like I said, I love the book's concept, the whole "I'm OK, you're OK" thing, very empowering for women and all, but it doesn't apply to me. I'm <u>not</u> OK. Really, I'm not!

— Daisy, 31

Daisy,

Obviously the "I'm not OK" stance is workin' for you, and I'd be loath to rip away that comfy security blanket of yours, but I've got to take issue with one point. You've decided you're too needy and clingy and that this horrible trait pushes guys away. Your Saran Wrap approach to relationships does you in every time, is that it?

Well actually, I bet you're right. I'm sure you're as needy as the day is long—a frickin' leech! I can see it now—a guy merely glances your way and you latch on like white on rice. And if your new "boyfriend" (as in some guy you talked to for five minutes at the bar last Saturday) doesn't call or text you ten times a day, you flip. I know your type. You're a lot of fun for guys, really.

So sure, I bet you do push *some* guys away. But those guys—well, they're the *wrong* guys, at least for you. See, I guarantee there are women right now in happy, loving relationships who are *way* more needy than you could ever be. They just happened to find their match and someday you will, too. It's really that simple.

So, cling away! In doing so, you'll naturally weed out the fellas who want a more independent woman and eventually, a guy looking for a needy, clingy, suck-the-life-outta-ya chick is gonna sop you up with a biscuit!

— Karin

The Awful Truth

The title of this section says it all. These scenes are not *based* on real stories. They *are* real stories!

WOMEN'S INHUMANITY TO WOMEN

CAST.

REBECCA: 37-year-old marketing director. Single.

ELLEN: 42-year-old freelance writer. Married with one child.

DEBBIE: 35-year-old stay-at-home mom with three children. On hiatus from a job in sales.

and It's Not Your Fault!

INTERIOR -- HOTEL BANQUET HALL - DAY

Rebecca, Ellen, and Debbie are attending a luncheon at the national convention of the Organization for Women Leaders and Entrepreneurs.

> ELLEN
> Hey, does anyone know if
> Audrey Landry was able
> to make it to convention?

> REBECCA
> No, I don't think she
> could come this year.

> DEBBIE
> That's too bad. I was
> hoping to catch up with
> her and make sure she's
> doing okay.

> REBECCA
> Okay? Last I heard she
> was doing great! She'd

23

just earned a big
promotion at work and
was headed to grad school
in the fall.

DEBBIE

Well, that's good to know,
but I was thinking more
about her personal life.
Things haven't been going
well. She never seems to
have a boyfriend and it
doesn't make sense.
She's so intelligent and
beautiful and fun to be
with!

ELLEN

Yeah, what's going on
with her? She's got to be
26 or 27 by now. You'd
think a girl like her would
have been snatched up
long ago!

24

DEBBIE

I can't figure it out either.
It's crazy that an
amazing woman like
Audrey isn't married
already! Too bizarre!
What's the problem?

REBECCA

Um, actually she's been
dating a guy for over a
year now and they just
moved in together.

ELLEN and DEBBIE let out a collective,
audible sigh of relief.

DEBBIE

Thank goodness! I really was
beginning to wonder what was
wrong.

Lesson Learned: Even among members of a
women's leadership organization—which by

definition is dedicated to the development of women per their career aspirations and entrepreneurial goals—the most important information about you is your relationship status. And your associates will be so concerned (read: obsessed) about it, they may gossip about you when you're not there and worse yet, in the presence of another member who happens to be older than you and further "off" the relational mark.

Guy Talk

Okay. Karin's totally right about the whole "you're fine just the way you are" thing and I've got the perfect example for you. I used to know this girl Abby, right? And let's just say she had a little junk in the trunk—and the back seat, and the passenger's side, and the dash, and the glove compartment, and the— (Okay, okay, we get it! — Karin) Anyway, she was always complaining about how guys only want

26

thin women and she'd go on and on about how men never asked her out and how they found her unattractive and immediately relegated her to the friend category. "Guys are so shallow! They only like the skinny chicks! I can't be anorexic, I already tried! Blah, blah, blah. . ."

Well, one day this new guy Rick starts working at my job. He's like a total partier and so he has this cook-out at his place a couple weeks after he got hired. So my buddies and I go over to throw a couple sausages on the grill or whatever. After a minute, I went inside to find his john—which was hard to do because I had to climb over all his crap 'cause this guy was a total slob. Anyway, I stumbled upon a box of old pictures and there's this hilarious shot of Rick all awkward in a tux and this girl in a prom dress with big hair and, let's just say, plenty of other big features, if you know what I mean. . . This little pictorial retrospective clued me in to his "preferences" when it comes to the ladies. I called Abby and invited her to meet up with us. The rest is history.

— Guy

Um, okay then. Well, personally I wouldn't have used that example but I've got to admit this story substantiates my point and, true, I did solicit a guy's perspective. . .

— Karin

Shout Out!

So to my smart, sexy, cream-of-the-crop, A-list, single friends I say this: You aren't screwed up, you don't need another self-help book, and no matter how much you pointlessly admonish yourselves, the whole deal is out of your control anyway. You're great women and you didn't mess anything up. There's nothing more you should or could be doing and nothing you need to change. You can't hurry love. It just hasn't happened yet.

chapter 2

It Just Hasn't Happened Yet and Your Mother Is Wrong!

you don't need to lose 10 pounds or wear a little more make-up

My mom always tells me that the good ones are getting snatched up left and right and I better get my act together before they're all gone. Doesn't she understand? I'd love to meet a nice guy and get married. All the pressure she puts on me doesn't help. It just makes me feel like I'm disappointing her and letting her down.
— Kendra, 30

Mothers. They mean well, of course, but wow, can they work our nerves! Even the most innocent interactions between a single daughter and her mom feel loaded with ulterior motives and hidden messages. Are we hypersensitive in assuming her every utterance contains oblique instructions as to how we might more readily procure a husband? Do our single daughter antennae detect criticism in seemingly benign advice and censure in innocent suggestions? Are we paranoid or is this our reality?

Certainly, I can't speak for the entire demographic, but a solid majority of mothers of single women spend a decent amount of time bemoaning their daughter's marital status. Since they're ruminating over our spinsterhood so much, they come up with countless explanations as to what we're doing to keep the gentlemen away. We're too independent or too dependent, too intimidating or too withdrawn, too aggressive or too passive, too opinionated or too shy. Too *something*.

Note also how the rules have changed since your younger days. When you were in high school, your mom called you "fast" for wearing too much black eye liner. Now she swears you'd meet a nice boy if you just put a little color on your cheeks. Back then, she encouraged you to choose your boyfriends carefully since none of the hoodlums you brought home was good enough for you anyway. Now, she claims you're too picky and pressures you to pursue every fool who glances your way. Then, she made you change your clothes if you tried to wear something too daring. Now, she insists you don't "doll up" enough.

And of course, there's always, "Whatever happened to that nice young man, Howie Johnston? He comes from such a good family and has a very bright future at the law firm. I know he was sweet on you. Why didn't you ever give him a chance? Honestly! If you think you're too good for everyone, you'll end up alone!"

We can't win, you know. Even if we have a boyfriend, we're still doing something wrong. We're with the wrong guy (again) so she commences with "Lecture Series A: Why You Keep Picking Liars and Losers". Or we're with the right guy (finally) and she proceeds to "Lecture Series B:

Selecting the Perfect Ultimatum to Make Your Boyfriend Propose". Naturally, both speeches are peppered with reminders about our ticking biological clock, warning that we're completely fooling ourselves if we think *in vitro* fertilization will solve everything, and besides, if we really loved her, we'd show a little concern for her lifelong desire for grandchildren. Somehow your brother's four kids don't count.

PSYCH 101: WHY SHE DOES IT

Remember, your mother operates with the mindset of another generation and another era. Sure, she made it to the new millennium, but her worldview harkens back a cool thirty or forty years. In my case, my mother represents the classic woman of the fifties—devoted wife and mother. She even majored in home-economics in college—yes, it was a real major at the time. And she began her senior year in the fall of 1957 terrified of reaching for a diploma at commencement with a ring-less left hand. Though just 21, she dreaded the thought of moving alone to a new town and embarking upon her teaching career as a single woman. People would pity her! And besides, how would she ever find a nice boy once she left college? Thankfully, just in the nick of time, she met my father and pulled off a "co-ed coup"— graduated in May and married in June.

Part of your mom's energy about your singleness could be a projection of how *she* would have felt if she were in your shoes. Many of our mothers couldn't have survived single. They just wouldn't have done it. They would have married anyone to avoid the stigma of being an "old maid"—a lovely moniker they'd have earned at the tender age of 25, by the way. I don't judge our mothers; theirs was a different era, after all. The pressure to marry and have children must have been overwhelming in the 1950s and 1960s. We still feel it today. Imagine what it was like then!

Your mom may also see your single status as a reflection on her parenting. Somehow, she must have failed you. At times, she questions and doubts herself—"How did I end up raising a spinster daughter! Where did I go wrong? Did I neglect to teach her the art of flirting? I knew I shouldn't have let her play soccer on the boys' team in second grade!" Parents begin to second-guess their child-rearing practices when things don't turn out as planned. Part of the reason she keeps rushing you to get married might be an attempt to let herself off the hook. Once you're wed, she can breathe a sigh of relief and feel assured she did a good job raising you.

Then again, if your mom hails from the baby-boom generation, she may pressure you for different reasons. She was no Donna Reed after all! Exactly the opposite, as a matter of fact. While you were growing up, she indoctrinated you in all things ERA, boasting of rallies, marches, and burned bras. Bedtime stories included excerpts from the writings of Gloria Steinem and Betty Friedan. Your mom declared you could do it all, have it all, and be anything you wanted *sans* a man. Please—by age 5, you knew you needed a man like a fish needs a bicycle.

But now, as you enter your 30s, she's starting to renege. Like the 1950s-era mother, she begins to question herself. "Maybe it's my fault. Did I have to force-feed her all that feminism? I'm sure I overdid it. I could have let her keep at least one of her Barbie's bikinis. And insisting that her Ken doll wear a 'Men are Pigs' t-shirt at all times was probably a little much." Looking back, she wonders if she did you a disservice. All that feminist rhetoric, while fun to toss around at book clubs and cocktail parties, won't keep you warm at night.

In addition, regardless of your mother's generation, she's probably experiencing a bit of peer pressure. That's right. Unfortunately, it survives long after high school. Very likely, your mom takes a hit or two about your singleness from various "friends" who see your maiden status as evidence that something is drastically wrong in your mom's perfect little family. These so-called friends may even enjoy seeing her obvious angst when discussing your husband-less existence. Heck, some probably look for opportunities to make her squirm. These women are the type who bump into your mom at the grocery store and immediately go for the jugular—*your* love life. "How's Jenny? Is she seeing anyone special?" Subtext: "Sure, things look good from the outside, but your daughter can't hang onto a man! Something must be frightfully wrong with her. Clearly, you're not such a great mother after all!" Of course, such women never ask your mom about your career, hobbies, travels, or volunteer work. They care about one thing: marriage. And until you're married, your mom has failed. Trust me, women can be catty at any age.

So when your mom puts the pressure on, remember, there may be a lot more behind it than you realize.

It just hasn't happened yet

Your mom's the control freak this time. And plenty of unfortunate fallout results from this way of thinking. First off, it's sad that your mom feels bad and that she imagines she's to blame for your singleness. That's quite a burden for her to carry around. Secondly, it's regrettable that her efforts to correct her misdoings involve offering you various suggestions as to how you could change yourself to find Mr. Right. Great tactic, because it leads to the third part of this sad situation. Now you feel bad because your mom criticizes you and implies something's wrong with you. Though she means well, the message remains, "You're flawed. Fix it. Find a man."

Ditto

Don't worry, help is on the way! Researchers in sociology and psychology are beginning to tackle the subject of single adulthood—even down to the part about single women and their nagging mothers!

"Mothers of single women over the age of thirty-five often impose the coupled ideal on their daughters. Today it is commonplace for a mother to brag about the educational accomplishments of her twenty-seven-year-old single daughter. But the mother of a fifty-year-old ever-single daughter often has very different feelings. She frequently says, 'I worry about Janet's being alone. I wish she would meet someone and settle down.' How often do we hear a mother say, 'I'm so proud of Janet; she bought her own home, won a teaching award last year, and has more friends than anyone I know'?"

— E. Kay Trimberger, sociologist and author of *The New Single Woman*

Girl Talk

Karin,

Let me just lay this out for you. This chapter may make sense for Gentiles, but clearly you don't understand the Jewish mother! Not only is it her <u>right</u> to find you the man of <u>her</u> dreams, but it's basically her entire reason for being! Oy! There's absolutely no getting through to her. Maybe some moms' behavior can be explained by this business about generational differences and middle-aged peer pressure, but a Jewish mother simply unloads any guilt she's feeling onto her daughter. Then, every time one of her fix-ups doesn't work out, she takes it as a personal affront to her match-making skills. She's plain ruthless!

From her perspective, I'm continually ruining my love life. She swears I'm too aggressive and that I need to let men take the lead. But the next thing I know, she's forcing me on some guy she wants me to meet and complaining I'm being too timid and not pursuing him enough. Then she nags me about my weight every time I see her, but gets all hurt if I don't take seconds and thirds of her brisket when I come over for dinner. And she never asks me about my job or my friends; all she can talk about is getting me married to a nice Jewish boy—SOON!

Oh, and by the way, his name is Howie Silverman, not Johnston, and my mother has never met *him, but he's the nephew of my parents' accountant and she's heard he's very handsome and very smart.*

— *Sarah, 34*

Sarah,

Shiksa that I am, I may have missed a few cultural nuances to the mom issue, but I've got to believe there's hope for *all* moms and daughters. Maybe your mom needs to read this chapter. A few times. And then a few more. Perhaps she should commit it to memory?

— Karin

The Awful Truth

Remember, these scenes are not *based* on real stories. They *are* real stories!

SHELF LIFE

CAST.

LISA: single 35-year-old restaurant
        manager
JOSEPHINE: her mother
ANTONIO: her step-father

INTERIOR -- ITALIAN RESTAURANT -
NIGHT

JOSEPHINE
As another year comes to
a close, I want to make a
toast to my hopes and
aspirations for my family.

ANTONIO
Oh, yes! Let's hear them!

JOSEPHINE
For my daughter, Lisa, a
toast to her finding the
husband of her dreams

who will bring her all the
happiness she deserves.

LISA
Oh, Mom, come on. You
know I'm perfectly happy.

JOSEPHINE
Maybe so, but you still
need a husband.

LISA
Yeah, well, I had one of
those and we saw how
that worked out.

JOSEPHINE
Lisa, you act as if you
don't ever want to be
married again!

LISA
Well, Mom, I'm not really
sure that I do.

Josephine freezes dramatically. She's unsure as to what to make of this.

JOSEPHINE
May I be frank here?

LISA
And when have you ever
not been frank, Mom?

JOSEPHINE
Honey, you really don't
know what you're talking
about. Sure, it's all fun
and games now because
you can live it up and
date a different man
every night. But you
have to realize this won't
last forever. Think about
it! You're only 35, so you
still look good now, but
how long do you really
think that's going to last?

43

Lesson learned: Single women have a shelf life. After about 35, our physical appearance deteriorates dramatically. So even if we're completely happy and content, we better lock in a husband because at some point in the future we may want one, but our looks will have expired and it'll be way too late.

Guy Talk

Listen. I'm obviously not a mother or a daughter and never will be. I think I'll pass the ball to my mom on this one. I've got a sister who just turned 30 and my mom's been pretty irritated with Karin recently for, as she puts it, brainwashing her.

— Guy

Mom Talk

Good, because I've got plenty to say on the subject. Honestly, Karin, I'd appreciate it if you stopped filling my daughter's head with all this nonsense—telling her she's fine just the way she is! If she were fine, she'd be married like all my friends' 30-year-old daughters. Please, what do you know? You're still single yourself, aren't you?

Now you listen to me. I love my daughter and I know what's best for her. And what's best for her is that she finds herself a nice husband to settle down with and start a family. And that's what she wants, too. You act like she's happy being single! She's not! She's very lonely.

45

And you could have been a little gentler with your treatment of mothers. Then again, you're not a mom so you can't possibly understand what it's like for us to watch our daughters go through heartbreak after heartbreak and get hurt time and time again. It's very painful for us! If we get a little pushy about finding the right guy, it's only because we worry so much. We're not getting any younger either, you know. Is it so wrong to want our daughters married and settled down before we die?

You think you're helping her with all this foolishness about her being fine the way she is, but that's not going to get her down the aisle any faster. In fact, it will probably slow things down.

She __needs__ to feel a sense of urgency. It'll help her get serious about getting her priorities straight and meeting her future husband!

—Guy's Mom

Guy's Mom,

Sorry, but I can't align with you on this one. You're saying you want your daughter happy, but I'm telling you, you're totally stressing her out with all the pressure you're putting on her! And as I mentioned in the chapter, you're also making her feel cruddy. Is that *really* what you want to do to her?

I know you think if she just got serious about finding a husband, she would. And you've probably nagged her to sign up for an online dating site or check out the church ice-cream social or maybe you've dropped a subtle hint at Christmas with a stocking full of "How to Nab a Man" self-help books.

I've got one word for you: STOP. Just stop it. Enjoy your daughter. Love her. Be grateful for her. Embrace every aspect of her—not just her marital status. She's fine just the way she is and one of these days, she'll meet him. It's just a matter of time.

That's right. She'll meet "The One" and rush home to introduce you to your future son-in-law. At first, you'll adore him. After all, he's the knight in shining armor come to rescue your princess from spinsterhood! Eventually, though, the newness will wear off and you'll wistfully think back to those precious days when you had your daughter all to yourself. Why? Because once you have a SON-IN-LAW, you become a MOTHER-IN-LAW. And we all know what that's about!

— Karin

P.S. As for the getting her settled down before you die thing? Look at it this way. If you truly can't depart this earth without seeing your daughter hitched, then apparently she's doing her part to keep you alive and kickin'!

Shout Out!

So to my smart, sexy, cream-of-the-crop, A-list, single friends I say this: You aren't screwed up, you don't need another self-help book, and no matter how much your mothers nag you, the whole deal is out of your control anyway. Your mothers didn't damage you. They're off the hook. And you? You're great women, and there's nothing more you should or could be doing and nothing you need to change. In this case, your mothers are wrong. It just hasn't happened yet.

chapter 3

It Just Hasn't Happened Yet and You're Not Too Picky!

you're choosing a life partner— aren't you supposed to be selective?

A single woman should accept herself for who she is and never bend down to anybody's standards. Follow your heart, and do what you know is right for yourself. And yeah, I've been called picky. But what should I do, pick up any Tom, Dick, or Harry off the street?
— Kimberly, 29

This one's a gem. *You're too picky.* Every woman I know who's been single for any period of time has heard it. If you haven't gotten it yet, you will. Just wait.

Be aware, it may come at you in another form. *You're too picky* can disguise itself in a comment like *You don't give guys a chance!* Or *You're awfully critical of the men you date!* Or *You really need to be more realistic!*

Realistic about what? What exactly are people trying to tell us? How are we supposed to take comments like this? Obviously, I'm on the receiving end of such statements, too, so I don't really know, but let's explore some plausible subtexts. "You're too picky" might mean:

- Apparently, you *think* you're pretty special, but you're no better than anyone else. It's time you considered lowering your stand-ards.

- You're no spring chicken! At this point, you need to be grateful for whoever you can get!

- Sure, I got to marry the love of my life. But that's not gonna happen for you. Sorry 'bout your luck!

- You must not see yourself clearly. You're aiming way out of your league. These homely sorts we set you up with are more your pace.

And these are our *friends* who say such things to us?

Let me get this straight. When you're 23, you're allowed to be picky. In fact, you're encouraged to select suitors carefully. Everyone tells you how smart, beautiful, and exceptional you are. You're a catch! You *should* be discriminating! But, as the years go on and you enter your 30s, people begin to chastise your choice to remain choosy. In fact, you've become a bit bothersome with your whole "I just want to wait for the right one" attitude. It's time to meet a guy, get married, and be done with it already!

How offensive and insulting to suggest that, because you're older than 25 or 35 or 45 or whatever arbitrary number someone designates as some sort of cut off, you need to be satisfied with whatever schmo comes your way! *Oops! I just celebrated my 36th birthday and everyone knows you can't be too picky after 35. So even though I used to hope for a smart, successful, charming guy, now I'll just set my sights on a dumb, unmotivated, boring guy.* Sure, that makes sense.

But single women aren't the only ones who have to field such comments. In fact, anyone remotely connected to us should take heed. Recently I learned my poor mother gets this little zinger, too. "Karin hasn't found anyone yet? Maybe she's being too picky. . ." Nice to know my marital status garners insults for both me *and* my mother. Knowing that women can be catty at any age (see Chapter 2), I have to wonder what's behind the "Your daughter's too picky" remarks mothers receive:

- I guess your daughter isn't quite the catch she thinks she is. She better go ahead and settle for whoever will give her a second look.

- Your daughter acts like she's hot stuff, but her arrogance makes her unattractive. Men don't go for women like that.

- You raised a little spoiled princess. Now look at the mess you have on your hands.

- Your snotty daughter thinks she's too good for anyone. It serves her right she's still single. Ha!

Okay, maybe there's no "Ha!" involved. . .

Psych 101: Why they do it

Honestly, I don't understand why anyone would encourage a woman to be less selective when choosing the person with whom she plans to spend the rest of her life. It seems like a pretty rotten idea all the way around. But let's assume most people have good intentions and are sincerely trying to help us. If that's the case, what might motivate the "you're too picky" comments?

In general, I imagine the "picky" slurs come from people who operate from a vastly different position than us. For instance, some women connect well with a wide array of men; they don't really have a "type". They love 'em all—jocks, stoners, surfers, suits, artists, nerds, sugar daddies, and boy toys. But perhaps you're the exact opposite. You know what works for you and don't want to waste time dating a homebody when your wanderlust will inevitably drive him nuts. Friends with a more equal-opportunity approach to dating might wonder why you pass up offers from decent guys. And because they're a bit more flexible in their selection process, they perceive you as picky.

Others might claim you're too picky because they're fixated on marriage. Those in this camp believe a woman hasn't "arrived" until she's donned the title of wife. Unable to comprehend an existence *sans* husband, they care little about whom we marry, just so long as we marry. To them, all guys are about the same anyway; just grab one and go with it. And perhaps they weren't all that picky themselves, so what's our problem?

Similarly, some women push marriage for the purpose of procreation. They *must* get married because they *must* be mommies. Reproduction is the ultimate goal and they intend to make it happen. No question. Therefore, when dating, this type of woman sizes up a guy primarily on his fathering potential. This quality might prove even more important than the romantic chemistry she has with her partner or how well they click as a couple. How she feels about her boyfriend holds less weight than how eager he is to hold babies at her family reunion.

Such women don't understand you're looking for more than just a baby daddy. They don't get it. So to them, you're just being too picky.

And by the way, that's fine—for them. No judgment for marrying whatever man for whatever reason. If a good-enough guy who'll provide a good-enough life is good enough, great! If he's got good-enough genes to make good-enough babies—good-enough! But, if you want a husband who's your best friend, best lover, and best partner, then by all means, be PICKY!

Finally, and this is a depressing one, but I suppose it's conceivable that in some instances, people call you picky because down deep they feel they settled and they hate watching you hold out for the right one. I don't like to think this way, but the possibility exists.

It just hasn't happened yet

Okay, for the sake of argument, let's say we ignore this chapter and admit to ourselves our friends are right. We hold up our hands, plead guilty and promise to knock it off. What, exactly, might happen if we single women stopped being so darn picky?

Well, if we go with the mindset that all guys are about the same and just take any old one, we'll probably find ourselves in lackluster marriages. Aiming the bar so low will likely cause us to feel superior to our spouses, introducing a dynamic of inequity into the relationship. That's always good for marriages, right? Best-case scenario, we pity our husbands. Worst-case scenario? We despise them and despise ourselves for settling.

Or, if the kid factor wins out, we might embark upon a marriage of convenience—partners in parenting, but nothing else. Since our marriage is all about the children, we might as well forget about romance and select someone who'll be a good father and a good pal. And those children we so desperately desired? They get to witness a loveless union—what a wonderful example to set for them! Best case scenario? Years of quiet desperation and extra-marital affairs. (Again, great familial baggage to dump on our kids.) Worst-case scenario? Divorce and a nasty custody battle. But at least we're mommies.

And by the way, how cruel is it to marry or even date a guy who thinks you're madly in love with him, who thinks he's the man of your dreams, when, actually, the only reason you're with him is that you *lowered your standards!* Best-case scenario? He lives a lie for 50 years. Worst-case scenario? He eventually realizes you never truly had it for him and leaves you for someone who will honestly love him. Or maybe that *is* the best case scenario. . .

Ditto

Right. We get it. We're super picky, super spoiled, stuck up little princesses, fully deserving of derision and disdain. Or maybe, just maybe, we're not complete and utter snobs, but rather, responsible women doing the right thing. Here's writer Leslie Talbot's take on the situation:

"As one of our nation's 90 million unmarried citizens, I've become inured to the social pressure to couple up—the backhanded insults and armchair psychoanalysis meted out by friends, co-workers, and well-meaning strangers at the bus stop whenever my marital status comes under scrutiny. And, believe me, I've heard it all. Selfish? Check. Immature? Check. Emotionally unstable? Check. Too picky for my own good? Check, check, and check.

But I've never bought into the prevailing notion that a perfectly fulfilling singular existence is little more than a karmic consolation prize. As far as I'm concerned, there's no more *un*fulfilling existence than one spent trapped with the wrong person. Take my word for it—a loveless marriage will sap your spirit and your sanity a lot more quickly than a lifetime of dateless Saturday nights. For me, then, and for many of the 41% of adults in this country who are single, singlehood is not merely the right choice. It is the responsible choice."

— Leslie Talbot, author, *Singular Existence: Because It's Better to Be Alone Than to Wish You Were*

Girl Talk

Karin,

I hate to break it to ya, but this chapter wasn't helpful at all. I used to be irritated when people told me I was too picky. Now I'm full-on offended! Thanks a lot!

But I do hear it all the time. My aunt tells me I'm too picky. My sister says it. So do the women at work. And you're right—our mothers get it, too. My mom told me her best friend never shuts up about how picky I am. Between you and me, though, I think she's just bitter because a few years ago she set me up on a date with her son, Jake. We went out a couple times *and he was a great guy—attractive, smart funny, and successful. But I just wasn't feelin' it, which was really too bad because he's a catch! Anyway, my mom's best friend has had an attitude with me ever since. And I guess in her head, I'm too picky because I wasn't into her precious baby boy.*

But to be honest, sometimes I do second guess myself. I wonder if I'm holding out for some ideal man who doesn't exist. I mean, what if I'm being unrealistic waiting for the fantasy of the perfect guy? A Prince Charming who looks like George Clooney but with Bono's bleeding heart, Bill Gates' brains, and Donald Trump's business sense? Am I kidding myself?

— Courtney, 28

Courtney,

First of all, when you meet that Prince Charming, please, *please*, *PLEASE* let me know if he has an identical twin brother 'cause that's got to be the perfect man!

But to answer your question—are you kidding yourself?—I don't think so. Look at it this way. You said yourself that Jake was a great guy and you *wish* you could have fallen for him because he would have given you a fantastic life. But I'm willing to bet that you *have* fallen for some guys in the past who weren't even the "catch" Jake was—guys who, on paper, pale in comparison to Jake but who "did it" for you, guys who had that indescribable quality that made you fall for them. After all, there's an element to attraction that can't be quantified. We can't put our finger on it, but we know it when we feel it. And we know when we *don't* feel it.

So give yourself a break. I doubt you're holding out for an unrealistic Prince Charming. But you are waiting for *your* Prince Charming. He may look more like Bill Gates than George Clooney (dang it!). He might have Bono's business savvy (well, he's pretty shrewd) with Donald Trump's hair (but really, that's got to be a toupée, right?). The point is, you'll fall in love because of your connection and chemistry. And any imperfections he has won't even faze you, because he's the one for you. Those deficits may have bothered other women he dated. Maybe they even broke up with him for those same flaws. But of course, they were being way too picky.

— Karin

The Awful Truth

Remember, these scenes are not *based* on real stories. They *are* real stories!

BEGGARS CAN'T BE CHOOSERS

CAST.

TRICIA: single 33-year-old school social worker

STEPHANIE: single 28-year-old 5th grade teacher

MARY PAT: smug teacher married for 15 years to "my husband, the lawyer"

INTERIOR -- BAR/GRILL - NIGHT

> MARY PAT
> So, ladies, how 'bout that
> waiter for one of you
> guys? He's a cutie.

> TRICIA
> Mary Pat, he's like 21!

> MARY PAT
> Well, maybe you're too
> old for him, Tricia, but
> Stephanie might be
> interested.

> TRICIA
> Steph, Mary Pat's decided
> I'm a dried up spinster
> and way too old for the
> waiter, but you could give
> it a shot. Whaddya
> think?

STEPHANIE
The waiter? Are you
kidding me? He's
obviously gay.

MARY PAT
Ugh! No wonder you girls
are still single. You're
way too picky!

Lesson Learned: If you're in your 30s and still
single, it's time to consider gay guys. Hoping for a
heterosexual constitutes being too picky. Besides,
you never know, you might "straighten" one out!

Guy Talk

Seriously, from a guy's perspective, Karin is
right on the money. I know women think men are the
cruel ones, but we actually get our little hearts broken
every once in a while. It's rough out there for us, too.

And the last thing we need is to start going out with some hot chick (who we kinda think is way out of our league, anyway) just to find out she's experimenting with being less picky about her dates and we're the lucky guinea pig. That's really uncool.

And I know what you're thinking: "Well, if I date down for a couple weeks, at least I've done a good deed. I've given some poor fool a moment of bliss with my goddess self." Look, that's no consolation. Leave us poor fools alone! That little moment with your goddess self could ruin us. Even if we only date you for a few weeks, we'll start thinking we can hang with your crowd. We'll be convinced we can play in the big leagues. We'll believe we're destined to date super-models all the time and we won't be satisfied with women we actually *can* date. So please, ladies, have a heart! Be picky!

— Guy

Wow. See why we need a guy's point of view? I would've never thought of any of that. But there you have it—straight from the source.

Apparently, it's not cruel to be picky; it's cruel to *not* be picky. I love it!

— Karin

Shout Out!

So to my smart, sexy, cream-of-the-crop, A-list, single friends I say this: You aren't screwed up, you don't need another self-help book, and no matter how much people try to tell you otherwise, you're *not* too picky. You are great women and you *should* be picky! There's nothing more you should or could be doing and nothing you need to change. And converting gay men isn't an option. It just hasn't happened yet.

It Just Hasn't Happened Yet and It's Not Because You Need to Get Back "Out There"!

rumor has it the "Land of Out There" is ripe with available men. . .

I'm tired of getting "out there". It hasn't done any good. Where I live it's hard to meet good guys anyhow. So I just quit every time.
— Leah, 34

Okay, first of all, you *are* out there. Unless, of course, you spend your days sequestered off from society, curled up in the fetal position, rocking back and forth chanting a *get-a-man-tra* of "Someday my prince will come." Come on! I'm out there, you're out there, we're all out there. Where else would we be?

Nevertheless I *know* you've heard this one. Getting back "out there" may be the most commonly provided explanation for why the unattached aren't dating. It's a particular favorite of happy couples, especially those who've been married for so many years they hardly remember being single. Smugly snuggled up in their suburban great rooms, they sip Diet Cokes and ponder the fate of their pitiful unmarried friends. "I can't believe Christa is still single! Why can't she meet a nice guy? There's got to be something she could do to meet desirable men!" They put their heads together, determined to ascertain an action plan to assist their solitary friend. Then, in a flash of insight, it comes to them. So simple, yet so profound. So brilliant, yet so facile. They can't wait to share the epiphany with their poor, lonely-hearted girlfriend! *She just needs to. . .* (drum roll, please) get back *"Out There"*.

How charming, too, that those who give us the get back "out there" pep talks are frequently people who never had to extend themselves whatsoever when trying to connect with the opposite sex. Their spouses simply fell into their laps. They met in graduate school or at the health club or in the waiting room at the dentist or at work or standing in line at the bank.

So just where, exactly, do our married friends imagine we are all day? And just what, exactly, do they think we're doing? From my observations, most single women engage in many of the same activities that brought love to their friends—they're attending graduate courses, working out at health clubs, sitting in waiting rooms at dentists' offices, going to work, and standing in line at the bank. But we haven't met him yet. So does that mean we need to get "out there" *more*?

And we do—to get "out there" *more*, we plan ladies' nights, don sexy little sandals and skimpy little skirts and hit the town. We make concerted efforts to see and be seen at the swankiest restaurants and hottest clubs. Sometimes we meet men. Sometimes we don't. And when we strike out, then what? All those big attempts to get "out there" *more* didn't work, so now what are we supposed to do? Have we not extended ourselves enough? Apparently not.

So we hurl ourselves out further and further, exploring more-creative options—speed dating, First Fridays, cooking classes, wine tastings, theater openings, charity benefits, and singles' cruises. The "out there" fever consumes us as a frenzied momentum builds. *Maybe my friends are right! Getting "out there" is gonna get me a man!* So thoroughly brainwashed by this balderdash, we begin to feel guilty for occasionally wanting to stay home for an evening. *I'm so tired from working all week. All I want to do is soak in the tub. But this could be the night I meet him! I'd never forgive myself for missing out on Mr. Wonderful just because I was too lazy to glam up and trip the light on a Friday night. Everyone says I need to get "out there"...*

Psych 101: Why they do it

This one goes back to the ever-present culprit—control. Your friends see that you're lonely sometimes. They know you get tired of going stag to weddings. They hear your horror stories and feel your pain. And as much as your peeps love you, they can't do a darn thing about it. If they could wave a magic wand and summon Mr. Right, they would in a second. But they can't. And they feel bad for you, which makes *them* feel bad.

And no one wants to feel bad 'cause that's no fun. So instead of sitting with the discomfort and admitting it stinks, they try to figure it all out. Swell idea, but what's to be done with circumstances completely out of their control? Nothing—except, of course, to tell you to get "out there". They comfort themselves thinking this sagacious suggestion will somehow solve your dilemma. Whew! Now they can feel better because they've given you the best advice they have.

As an added bonus, it kind of takes them off the hook. Because if you don't get "out there" enough (*enough* being whatever subjective standard they've set), they won't have to feel sorry for you anymore—"I told her to get 'out there' more, but she doesn't! What's the matter with her?" Pity morphs into blame because you're clearly responsible for your solitary state. You're just not getting "out there" enough!

None of this is intentional, of course. Your friends don't ever say to themselves, "It pains me to see Britney all alone. I know she hasn't had a boyfriend in a while and she'd like to be dating someone. She's hurting and that makes me feel bad. Hmm. I sure don't want to feel bad. . . I know what I'll do! I'll give her a lame idea to get 'out there'! That way, I've done my part. And if she doesn't take me up on my advice, well then, that's on her. Good deal! I sure hope this works, because I'd really like to stop feeling sorry about her lack of a love life. I'm actually getting rather irritated with her about it."

It just hasn't happened yet

Well, as noted previously, someone's got to take the blame for your single status, right? And once again, you're the fall guy. If you'd only position yourself more effectively and truly commit to finding a man, it would happen. Use a little strategy, for goodness' sake! Launch yourself into every conceivable male milieu. Perform daily operations in husband hunting. Get serious about the pursuit and it will all work out.

Once again, you get the message you're doing something wrong. It's your fault you're single. If you'd just get off your tush and make an effort, you'd meet him. It's time to get intentional about this, darn it! Get back "out there"!

Nice. It sure feels good to get blamed for something you already feel cruddy about but can't change. In their attempts to help, friends end up making things worse. Sure it's unintentional, but that's what happens.

Ditto

Sociologist E. Kay Trimberger's research challenges the effectiveness of strategies like getting "out there". For over twenty years, Trimberger has studied unmarried women, chronicling the vicissitudes of navigating single life in a couples' world. Her participants represent the gamut—women who have made peace with their status and those who continue to pursue marriage. Trimberger notes that a relentless quest for coupledom may be related to a reduction in life satisfaction. Through observations and interviews, she has found that those single women who put the *most* energy and effort into trying to find a partner appear to be the *least* happy. So, although offered with the best of intentions, those "you just need to get back out there" pep talks from your friends and family might be the least helpful suggestion they could give.

Girl Talk

Karin,

Oh my gosh! If I had a quarter for every time one of my happily married friends has given me the "You gotta get out there" pitch, I'd be a millionaire! I just wanna smack 'em!

Take my friend, Lauren. She's the worst offender—especially since she has absolutely no idea what she's talking about. She serial-dated throughout college and then landed a fluff job as a receptionist at a law firm. Within a month she began seeing this young, hotshot attorney. Six weeks later, she moved in with him. Fast forward four years, and they're married.

The best part is, she constantly reminisces about her lonely post-college single days, and she acts like she's <u>finally</u> settling down after years of tearing up the town with her Holly Golightly self. But it's not like you're really single if you have a serious boyfriend and you live with him! Give me a break!

But, like I said, she's the one who preaches the "out there" message non-stop. It's always, "Jill, you're never going to meet a man if you only hang out at gay bars singing show-tune karaoke! I know you pride yourself on being a fruit fly, but flitting around with fairies won't get you a husband! You gotta get where the action is. You know what you should do? Check out some of the bars downtown where the traders go for happy hour. . ."

As if she knows the first thing about being single! All she did was show up to work one day and score herself a junior partner. Did she have to get "out there" to meet her man? I don't think so.

Am I wrong to be a little bitter?

— Jill, 32

Jill,

I don't hear bitterness—I hear you stating the facts. What's most irritating about Lauren is that she thinks she's an expert on what you're going through when, clearly, she has no clue. If she did, she'd realize just how insensitive she is with her "out there" solution. All the single women I know *hate* when they hear this ridiculous "solution". So, you've got a point—she was never really single. At least not single the way you're single.

And by the way, gay bars are a single girl's best friend! What's better than a room full of beautiful boys, who can actually sing karaoke *and* will talk to you without looking you up and down, unless it's to compliment you on your fashion-forward ensemble, of course. They never approach you with tacky pick up lines, and they love dishing on all the same stuff you do—pop culture, celebrity gossip, and interior design. Plus, they always have the word on which stylists do the best highlights—and that's *priceless* information. At a gay bar you can totally be yourself because no one ever mistakes your friendliness for flirtation; no mess, no fuss, no confusion (except for when the bisexuals show up and throw us all off, but that's another story). Again, if Lauren had actually been single for a while, she would know the haven that is the gay bar and the joy of "straight-girl/gay-boy" love.

— Karin

The Awful Truth

Remember, these scenes are not *based* on real stories. They *are* real stories!

DOUBLE BIND

CAST.
KATE: single, 25-year-old graduate student
BARB: her mother

INTERIOR -- KATE'S CITY APARTMENT - DAY

Kate is on the phone with her mother, who lives in a nearby suburb.

BARB
So, honey, do you have
any good news for me?

KATE

Mom, if you're referring
to my love life, then, no, I
suppose I don't.

BARB

[sighs] Well, I guess I
really shouldn't expect
any new developments
since you're making
absolutely no effort to
meet anyone!

KATE

[exasperated]
Unbelievable! You think
I'm not trying?

BARB

No, I certainly don't think
you're trying. I don't see
you doing anything at all
to meet men. I've told
you before, you've got to
extend yourself a bit,

Kate. Get back "out
there"! Guys aren't going
to just come knocking on
your door!

KATE
For your information,
Mom, I AM extending
myself. Do you want
details? Let me break it
down for you—in the last
couple weeks I've joined
two match making
websites, attended a
speed-dating event, went
to a singles' cooking class
and signed up to play co-
ed softball through the
Chicago Social Network.

BARB
You mean to tell me
you've done all that and
you haven't met even one
nice boy?

KATE

Yes, Mom. That's exactly
what I'm telling you.

BARB

Oh, for heaven's sake,
Kate. If that's the case
then you must be doing
something wrong. You're
probably coming across as
way too desperate!

Kate slams down the phone.

Lesson Learned: It's *always* your fault. *Always!* If
you heed the "get back out there" mandate without
success, then obviously you messed it up. You've
gone out *too* far or got lost and ended up in the
wrong *there.* Or something.

Guy Talk

"Out there", huh? Is that where we guys are supposed to be? I'm gonna assume you're looking for a dude like me, which might be a stretch, I know, but I'm here to give the guys' perspective so. . . And I don't know where I am exactly, but I can definitely say I'm not "out there" and neither are my guy friends. We're just living our lives and doing our thing. We're going to the dentist and the bank and all those other places Karin said single women go. Although I haven't seen a hot chick at the dentist since I was 12 when I had this huge crush on the hygienist at my orthodontist's office. Wait, does that count? Anyway, she was always leaning over and bracing herself against me when tugging at my wires. It was so hot! I used to eat popcorn on purpose just to try to break my braces so my mom would have to schedule appointments. . . (Um, could ya get back to the point? —Karin) Right, the point is, I can't tell you exactly where to go to meet us, but we're around and we're looking. In fact, a lot of us are just like you; we're keeping an eye open for a love connection if one should happen to walk by.

But as for the gay bars? Karin's way off here. First of all, Lauren is right. Straight guys *don't* go to gay bars, so Jill will never meet potential marriage material there. Secondly, "fruit flies" (is that the new PC term?) are a total turn off to straight men. It's way too intimidating to date a woman with a lot of gay friends. I mean, how can we compete with those guys? They're good listeners, for Pete's sake! They actually *enjoy* all the foolish minutiae women bore us with when telling a story. Plus, they rarely audibly belch! And they send cards and flowers for birthdays and anniversaries whereas straight men are lucky if they even remember the dates in the first place. They spoil their "girlfriends" and all this does is ruin it for straight guys 'cause women start becoming accustomed to all this attention.

I dated a "fruit fly" once and it was a nightmare. She constantly compared me to all her "gay boyfriends", and of course, I *always* came up short. No, I don't wear tight designer jeans. No, I don't care about last week's episode of *Gossip Girl.* And no, I don't want to manscape!

— Guy

Well, obviously we part ways on this one. I recognize that the natural affinity between gay men and straight women rarely translates to gay men and straight men, but what's with the hostility? Can't we all just get along?

— Karin

Shout Out!

So to my smart, sexy, cream-of-the-crop, A-list, single friends I say this: You aren't screwed up, you don't need another self-help book, and no matter how much you get "out there", the whole deal is out of your control anyway. You are great women—just keep living your fabulous lives, hanging where you normally hang and doing what you normally do. There's nothing more you should or could be doing and nothing you need to change. Where exactly is "out there" anyway? It just hasn't happened yet.

chapter 5

It Just Hasn't Happened Yet and It's Not Because You Need to "Tone It Down a Notch"!

um, are we living in 1895?

What strikes me about all the advice we get, especially the pat phrases, is how anti-feminist it is. What they're really saying is, "You're not acting in a feminine enough way. Be prettier! Be more passive! Don't be so much yourself; only demure girls get men—and you're nothing if you don't have a man." Meanwhile, everything I've read from the gripe tripe of pop-psych to more meaty scientific articles suggests that single women suffer far less than single men. They tend to need us a lot more than we need them. I think women are pressured to attach themselves to men partly because of that

> *and partly because having a male partner is seen as a sign of social accomplishment. It's not really about what a woman needs emotionally.*
>   — Anne, 38

You've come a long way, baby! Be anything! Be everything! You can have it all! Stretch, grow, excel, shine! Nothing's holding you back! Reach for the stars! Play among the stars! *Be* a star!

At least, that's what they told us when we were little.

So we did. Lived our lives to the fullest, exceeded our potential in every area, all the while basking in the praise of friends and family cheering from the sidelines: "Look at her go!" "So ambitious! So accomplished!" "We couldn't be prouder!"

And they were—proud of us, that is. Until we ran into some trouble achieving the most critical and crucial of womanly pursuits—the hunt for a husband. Then they changed their tune:

- "Hmmm. . . Still single at 30. I'm wondering if you intimidate men."

- "Well, you're pretty opinionated. A lot of guys might find that to be a bit much."

- "Of course, you do have a lot of degrees. Most men don't want a wife who's more educated than they are."

- "You know, men marry down and women marry up. You've worked yourself into a situation where there aren't too many men left in the tiers above you."

- "I'm not saying you should 'dumb it down' or anything, but maybe rein things in a bit so guys won't feel so threatened by you."

So after years of profuse encouragement to reach, soar, strive, and achieve, now we hear we need to "tone it down a notch". Seriously?

Oh yeah, they're serious. And we better get with the program if we think we're ever going to find our way to the altar. Wake up, ladies! All that grrrl power flies at sorority conventions and book clubs, but we better keep it under wraps when in the company of eligible bachelors—at least if we hope to appear appealing to said eligibles. Because, apparently, over the last 50 years as women gained equality, men missed the memo.

Well, okay, to be fair, some men got the memo, and indisputably the social climate in the latter part of the twentieth century ignited profound changes for both sexes. Gender expectations relaxed and women began to revel in myriad opportunities—so much so that currently more women complete college than men. And in many graduate programs and professions, females lead the way. Gone is the time when the apex of a woman's existence consisted of squeezing into a torpedo bra, whipping up fondue in high heels, and washing down an insipid, identity-stifling suburban-housewife life with "mother's little helpers".

So, clearly, we represent liberated women of the new millennium, right? Our generation escaped the confines of female role-entrapment. The gender revolution of the 1960s and 1970s brought forth a new day, providing women with infinite opportunities and the freedom to pursue their true, genuine selves. The women's movement hit, and all the sexist rules got thrown out the window. Or so we thought.

Psych 101: Why they do it

Apparently, some of those rules fell a few feet shy of the window and got neatly swept under the rug. Now surreptitiously out of sight, they remain, arguably, more powerful and difficult to tackle in their covert state. And the most persistent of these dictates? The ones pressuring us to partner. Because no matter how successful and accomplished and brilliant a woman is, she's still a failure without a man. Period.

No one admits it outright—that would be so last millennium—but subverted, biased ideation clutches white-knuckled to our collective consciousness, so cleverly that we often remain oblivious to our own bigoted positions—until the sneaky sexism comes up for air, outing itself in directives such as "Tone it down a notch" or "Be careful! Don't intimidate men or you'll never get one."

Often, however, it manifests more subtly, creeping circuitously into our explanations of relationship demise: "Well, they were both up-and-coming attorneys, but she eventually made partner and he didn't. If you ask me, it took a huge toll on them. That's when things turned south." Or, "You know, she had a slew of boyfriends in college, but she's very driven. And how many men want a wife who works 12 hour days?" Or, "Sure, she's ambitious and attractive, but Jim's not the kind of guy who planned on competing with his wife's career—or with his wife!" Or, "She's so quick-witted and super smart. You could tell it bothered him; he felt upstaged all the time."

Sadly, these scoldings come not only from those with "old school" ideology, but also from peers and contemporaries—our "girls". Sexism is alive and well, concealed from view, but still wielding its potency.

Naturally, those who say these things are just trying to help. And obviously, they fail to think through their reasoning before spewing such inane counsel. If people actually reflected for a moment, could they possibly believe anyone benefits from one member of a relationship essentially faking it by presenting a watered-down version of herself?

Ditto

A clear expression of the "tone it down" sentiment surfaced as a cautionary statistic in the now famous 1986 Newsweek article which declared a single, 40-year-old college educated woman was more likely to be killed by a terrorist than ever get married. Twenty years later when Newsweek admitted the inaccuracy of the data, many writers like Kira Cochrane responded strongly: "Let's face it, this notion, with its brilliant conjunction of loneliness and violent death, always seemed pretty suspect. Nonetheless, the statistic gained stunning popularity. As the perfect, doom-laden warning to all us pesky women who insist on, you know, enjoying ourselves, getting educated and developing a career before settling down, it has become one of the most repeated statistics of all time. [If you] spotted a single thirty-something woman having fun? Just warn her that she has more chance of being bombed than getting anyone to love her and commit to her. That'll wipe the smile off her face!"

Writer Lynn Harris also spoke to the Newsweek retraction, focusing on "one of the 14 then-doomed singles interviewed in 1986. Guess what? She got married at 40 and remains blissfully so at 50. 'I've watched a lot of people [who married while young] get divorced,' she says. 'I think that if you do wait until Mr. Right comes along, you have a much better chance of survival.'"

So how 'bout some valid research on the subject? Economist Heather Boushy analyzed U.S. survey data of over 33 million women and found that high achieving women are no less likely than average working women to be married or have children by age 40. Apparently, they didn't "tone it down a notch" and they got it all.

It just hasn't happened yet

No question—though we live in a post-feminism era, residual, archaic conceptualizations of women's value and worth persist. So where does that leave us?

If we made the "mistake" of believing we should reach our fullest potential and we did, in fact, accomplish, acquire, and achieve, we may now learn we've painted ourselves into a mate-finding corner, albeit an impressive and remarkable corner, but a corner nonetheless. So "up" we have nowhere to go but "down". Our choices? Take their advice and rein ourselves in a bit or carry a mantle of "To thine own self be true" and instead of searching for partners above us, take a look at those below. Wow. Both options sound so very enticing.

But what's even more troubling to me is our response. They warn us to "tone it down" and sometimes, in our weaker moments, we actually consider it. We crack. We cave. We concede and wonder if they've got a point. Why? Because we, too, fail to appreciate the power of these unseen, antiquated notions pressing upon our psyches and asserting their influence, causing us to doubt and question our very selves. Supposedly, we've come a long way, baby. Yeah, right.

Girl Talk

Karin,

"Tone it down a notch" is the worst! Whenever I hear it I always get furious at the idiot who had the

nerve to say it. If repressing a part of who I am is what it takes to get a guy, then I'm happy to write off marriage all together. I want a husband who can keep up with me, not drag me down, and I have no intentions of settling. The sky's the limit, and I can take care of myself!

But here's what I want to know. Do men ever get this garbage? I mean, if a guy is 35 and single, do his family members pull him aside at Christmas parties and suggest that the reason he can't find a girlfriend is because he's just a bit "too much" for women to handle? Do they make him doubt his great, gutsy qualities or encourage him to be anything less than who he is? Of course not! It's appalling that people feel perfectly comfortable saying such offensive things to women that I know for a fact they'd never utter to a man. What's that all about, anyway?

Someone once told me that American women are the most liberated in the world. I'm kinda doubting it.

— *Alex, 27*

Alex,

I agree. No argument here. Do guys get this stuff? Definitely not! They've certainly got their own junk to deal with (and I'm sure Guy will clue us in on it shortly) but it's not the same. And if you ask me, we get it way worse. Maybe I'm not being sensitive enough to the guys' perspective but, hey, some dude can write a book for them.

— Karin

The Awful Truth

Remember, these scenes are not *based* on real stories. They *are* real stories!

TOO MUCH IS NEVER ENOUGH

CAST.
ANGELA: single 38-year-old college professor

99

MONA: Angela's aunt, whom she rarely
        sees
LOIS: married 37-year-old stay-at-home-
          mom. Angela's cousin and
          Mona's daughter

EXTERIOR -- COMMUNITY PARK - DAY

The family is gathering for its annual reunion. Angela is home for the first time in
several years. Angela, Mona, and Lois
stand together eating brownies.

> MONA
>
> [to Lois] Now would you
> look at Angela? Is she a
> catch or what? I can't
> imagine why she's not
> taken! What are those
> men missing? Can't they
> see it?

LOIS

[embarrassed] Please,
Mom, what are you
talking about? Of course
men see it! I'm sure
Angela is just being
discriminating—as she
should be!

MONA

[to Angela] No seriously,
how is it that a man
hasn't snatched you up?

Angela laughs uncomfortably.

ANGELA

Oh, you know, Aunt
Mona. I just keep flitting
away! They can't pin me
down!

Mona's eyes widen and she nods with
understanding.

MONA

Of course! That's it!
You're just too much for
them! So brilliant! So
talented! So beautiful!
They wouldn't even know
what to do with you.
Really, I'm sure most
men just can't keep up!

ANGELA

Well, I don't know about
that. . .

MONA

And we all know how men
are. They've got to feel
like they're in charge and
they certainly wouldn't
with you. I get it now,
like I said, you're just too
much for them.

                    LOIS
          Great, Mom. Real
          encouraging.

                    MONA
          Well, sure it's
          encouraging! Now we
          understand what the
          problem is.

                    LOIS
          I'm not sure anyone
          thought there was a
          problem in the first place,
          Mom! Could you just
          leave her alone already?

Angela quietly makes an escape while Lois
and Mona's arguing escalates.

Lesson Learned: If you're perceived as a "catch"
but haven't been "caught" people may formulate
explanations concerning the *immensity* of you.

I'm not quite sure if this speaks to your personality, intellect, abilities, accomplishments, presence, aura, emanations, subtle body or what. But somehow, in some way, you're just too much! You're so great and it's making everyone else feel bad, especially the guys, so can't you tone it down a notch already?

Guy Talk

My only reaction to this chapter is a resounding, *Huh?* I mean, Karin makes a strong case for the reasons behind this kind of lame advice, but I still don't get it.

For one thing, I can't figure out what exactly you women are supposed to "tone down". And I'm totally clueless about this business of being "too much" or "too threatening" because the vast majority of guys I know love spunky women. As a matter of fact, I hear way more complaints from my friends about girls being passive and boring. You know the whole, "Where do you want to go for dinner tonight?" And all he ever hears is, "I don't care. You pick." Now _that_ will drive a man crazy and drive him away. But a woman with a brain and some attitude? Please, the guys are gonna be all over her. Don't you know men love nothing more than a challenge?

Oh, and while we're on the subject, lean in and listen closely. Guys HATE when women are phony. We despise it in every way, shape or form, except for a small subset of us who like the phony things that result from certain surgical procedures, if you know what I mean. (Seriously, Guy? — Karin) Hey, I said it was a minority of us. . .

Anyway, I can tell you for a fact that I've heard plenty of talk over beer and brats about how this or that chick plays games and is full of crap and is never straight-up about anything. Trust me. By the end of that conversation, every guy at the table detests that girl.

So, I gotta say, I think "toning it down" is probably some of the worst advice a woman could get. It would most likely backfire because if a guy senses

that a woman is trying to be anything other than
herself, he's gonna bolt. No questions asked.

— Guy

Veni. Vidi. Vici.

— Karin

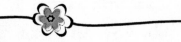

Shout Out!

So to my smart, sexy, cream-of-the-crop, A-
list, single friends I say this: You aren't screwed
up, you don't need another self-help book, and you
better not tone down even one tiny ounce of
yourself. Your fabulousness is a gift to the world!
You're great women and you didn't mess anything
up. There's nothing more you should or could be
doing and nothing you need to change. Go ahead
with your bad self. It just hasn't happened yet.

It Just Hasn't Happened Yet and It's Not Because You're Not Trying Hard Enough!

so don't feel obligated to go on every fix-up, set-up, and blind date that's thrown your way

Being single while almost everybody else is married can sometimes be a little tough, especially when all your married friends try to pair you up with anybody they believe would be a good partner. What's stressful is when you don't feel like going out with the guy and they feel you're being too picky. I get mad, but then I think, "If I don't try harder I might be alone

forever!"   But is love supposed to feel like
pulling teeth or running a marathon?
— Denise, 32

"You're not trying hard enough." I wish I could chalk this criticism up to urban mythology, but, no, it's legit. In fact, I'm merely one degree of separation from a story confirming its existence. Here goes. Recently divorced and back in the singles' scene, my friend, Tracy, was surprised at how tough it was to meet quality men. At lunch with her mom and aunt one day, she began lamenting the challenges of dating after eight years off the market. But her Aunt Judy wasn't having it. "I don't know how you can even complain! What have you done to meet someone? Nothing! We have so many friends with nice, eligible sons, but you refuse to let us set you up. No wonder you're single! You're just not trying hard enough!"

True, in the vast majority of life's endeavors, increased effort equals increased probability of success. No need for dispute. But for every rule there's an exception, and, unfortunately, finding

"The One" simply doesn't fit the *"effort = success"* equation. Because, trust me, there are a lot of women giving it all they've got but still coming home empty-handed night after night.

Furthermore, what exactly constitutes trying hard *enough*? Who determines the level of acceptable effort? All the single women I know make regular and concerted overtures to meet men. We seek out occasions to interact with available bachelors all the time! We frequent hipster bars and coffeehouses, take our puppies to dog parks and our cats to hot, unattached veterinarians. We even buy groceries on "singles' night" at *Whole Foods*. What more do we have to do to convince our friends, family, coworkers, and whoever else weighing in on the issue that we're trying as hard as we possibly can?

Well, according to Tracy's Aunt Judy, you just need to let 'em set you up. Acquiesce. Give in. Put on your game face and accept that blind date with your grandmother's neighbor's brother's lawyer's step-son's best friend. You might as well concede. They'll badger you incessantly until you comply. You'll never win this battle, anyway. The opponent comes too well prepared! Armed with abundant folklore and old wives' tales, they weave elaborate yarns about women who met the loves of their lives on random fix-ups. And if you'd just try a little harder, it could happen for you, too!

Granted, set-ups have probably garnered a few happy matches over the last millennium, yet for every such instance, there are a million (or at least several thousand) disastrous scenarios. Mostly because when folks set us up, they simply don't think. Or, if they are thinking, they employ severely wacked reasoning. "Let's see, I have a single friend who is male. And I have another friend who is single and female. She's extroverted, outdoorsy, and a world traveler. He's introverted, prefers his computer to people, and at 35, has yet to leave his home state. Look at that! How fantastic! A match made in heaven! They'll live happily ever after for sure!"

I know they're only trying to help, but is it so hard to see that most of the time we have *nothing* in common with the men they pick? As if the only criteria necessary for compatibility is complementary genitalia. *"He = man"; "she = woman"*. A perfect fit!

Then again, even if the guy *is* a halfway decent match for us, we may still shy away from the set-up, if we're smart. Why? Because letting a friend play Cupid is one of the most precarious dynamics you can introduce into your relationship. It's horribly risky! The pressure! The expectations! This seemingly innocent and supportive gesture can devastate your friendship.

Think about it. Essentially, a set-up presents a lose-lose situation for you and your matchmaking friend, unless, of course, you fall madly in love with Bachelor #1 the minute you lay eyes on him. If that happens, I'll take it all back because, clearly, that's a win-win (except that your girlfriend will feel entitled to be the maid of honor in your wedding, as a sort of finder's fee, and that might tick off your sister. . .) But anything short of love at first sight can lead to friendship fallout.

Let me explain. If, after the blind date, you decide you're not into him, be advised, your friend's going to take it personally. She'll say it's cool, of course, but that's a lie. In actuality, she'll be extremely upset and the closer her relationship with the guy, the more miffed she'll be. If it's her brother, watch out. It could completely ruin your friendship because by rejecting him, you're rejecting her. She may even lash out and tell you you're *too picky*! (See Chapter 3 for assistance.)

But what about the flip side? There's always the possibility that you'll find the guy appealing, but he won't be "feelin'" you. That's no fun, either. Again, potential friendship fallout. Since in this case you're the one who's smitten, you'll be chomping at the bit to find out what he thought of you. You may even start stalking your friend, calling her ten times a day to see what sort of impression you made. Meanwhile, she's performing elite mental gymnastics to find a way to let you down gently. Now she feels bad about coming up with the whole idea and you're angry and humiliated. *Voila!* A barrier in the midst of what used to be a perfectly decent friendship.

Clearly, if we're smart, we may steer clear of set-ups altogether—especially ones orchestrated by those close to us. After all, who wants to jeopardize a good friendship on the miniscule chance that the matchmaking might manufacture something special?

PSYCH 101: WHY THEY DO IT

They do it because they don't know what else to do. They say it because they don't know what else to say. Falling back on what they *do* know, the old equation of *"effort = success"*, they take a stab at it on our behalf in the form of a horribly hapless fix-up. Or maybe they're speaking from experience. Perhaps they were single once and tried really, really hard and let themselves get set up five times a week for five years and then finally met someone wonderful. Lucky them! Sometimes that happens. Sometimes it doesn't. But love isn't math, and there are no formulae and no algorithms. And actually, trying has *nothing* to do with it.

Know that, even though it hurts when they say we're not trying, they don't mean to hurt us. Know that they're frustrated for us, not with us. Know that the insult of a ridiculously incompatible match is unintended. They just want to help. If they could change things, they would. And of course, they can't, so they say stupid things sometimes, like "you're not trying hard enough," and do stupid things other times, like fixing us up with guys we'd never be interested in. Hey, at least they didn't tell us to get back "out there"!

It just hasn't happened yet

As noted, blind dates and set-ups almost always involve painful emotional aftermath. Since these contrived meetings rarely work, more often than not, both parties leave disappointed and hurt. And *yes*, I mean both parties.

For example, let's say you've been set up with this guy, John. Both of you have been single for a while, so naturally, both of you approach the date with a bit of cynicism and low expectations. However, much to his surprise, John finds you to be attractive, intelligent, funny, and entertaining. And though you recognize that John, too, is attractive, intelligent, funny, and entertaining, you don't feel that "spark" or romantic connection. You therefore spend the entire date trying to remain polite and attentive, while not encouraging John. After dessert, you part ways and go home to lick your wounds.

John's injury is obvious. He feels rejected and disappointed. It hurts when romantic interest isn't reciprocated.

But you did the rejecting so you should leave unscathed, right? Wrong. Because though it was just one date, which you approached with much skepticism, still down deep a tiny, little part of you ignited a flicker of hope that he could be "The One" and things might actually work out for once. Sigh.

Yet far more deleterious shrapnel from the post-blind-date fallout entails the analyzing and second guessing yourself. *He was such a nice guy. I really wish I could've been attracted to him. He's got a great job, he's cute, and he cracked me up the whole time. What's my problem, anyway? Maybe I am too picky, like everyone says. Maybe I do think I'm too good for anybody. Maybe I'm a raging narcissist, basking in delusions of grandeur, destined to forever refuse every perfectly decent man who comes my way!* You started the evening feeling single and lonely. You leave it feeling single and lonely *and* callous, mean, and unsure of yourself.

No one seems to understand any of this when they pressure us to pair up with every random recommendation we receive. See, I told you—both parties leave disappointed and hurt.

Ditto

Audrey Irvine, senior assignment manager for CNN, shared this snippet in a *Relationship Rant*, which she writes for CNN.com:

"Enter exhibit A: Female, 40 years old, single, career woman, no kids, victimized by 10 unsuccessful 'hookups' per year since the age of 35... I remember going to a barbecue where I didn't realize I was one of the entrées for another single man in attendance. Somewhere between eating potato salad and rocking out my best Beyoncé moves in the karaoke competition, it came to light that my friend thought this 'gentleman' and I were meant to meet.

As I wiped my sweaty brow and gazed at him in his circa-1970s outfit, I realized I had just auditioned for this guy. That's when I asked my friend what she possibly thought I had in common with this man outside of us both having a pulse. She had no answer except that we were both single. Shared interests, mutual attraction? Those got no consideration."

Girl Talk

Karin,

Absolutely. Definitely. I second the motion, etc., etc., etc. You're right about all this stuff, but you forgot the other annoying thing about matchmaking— when your friends talk up some guy and promise to introduce him to you and then never deliver!

This happens to me all the time! One of my friends will be like, "I've got the perfect guy for you," and then she'll go on and on about how fantastic he is and make me promise to meet him at a party or fundraiser or whatever. And at first I'll be a little dubious, but after an hour and a half of hearing how great he is, I'll get intrigued and want to see for myself.

But a week later I'm still waiting to hear the details on how I'm supposed to meet the guy. Do you think that party invitation ever arrives? NO! Does the Evite for the benefit show up in my inbox? Of course not! My girl goes back to her comfortable married life and forgets all about the fact that she made me fall madly in love with some guy I don't even know! Not nice!

And the best part is — these friends are the same ones who have the NERVE to tell me I'm not trying hard enough to meet men.

— Janelle, 31

Janelle,

Dang. That's harsh. *You're* not trying hard enough, but *they* can't even make a phone call and arrange a double date? I feel your pain, girl. It's happened to me. It's happened to my single friends. We've all been there.

In fact, a few years ago my happily married brother persuaded my friend Kelly that she and his buddy *had* to meet each other. My brother spent an entire Sunday afternoon convincing her that they were destined to be together, Kelly and Kyle—a match made in heaven. And since she was single and pretty lonely at the time, she glommed onto the idea with a vengeance. She was like, "You know, it's crazy. I couldn't pick him out in a crowd, but I've got a hunch I'm gonna marry that Kyle Miller. I can feel it!" Sure, she was joking (kinda), but after all the hype, she wanted to at least meet him.

But do you think that rendezvous ever happened? You know it didn't. My brother's ADHD bounced him onto the next topic or person or whatever else was going on in his life and Kelly never heard another peep about her sure-to-be future husband.

You're right. It's not nice. But someone else has to write that book and let the marrieds know. Some sort of "How to" book, maybe—*How to Not be a Jerk to Your Single Friends* or *How to Avoid Getting Your Girl's Hopes Up* or *Please Shut Up About That Great Guy If You're Just Going to Go Back to Your Happily Married Life and Never Actually Introduce Us to Him Anyway*. Okay, that last title wasn't the catchiest, but you get the idea.

— Karin

The Awful Truth

Remember, these scenes are not *based* on real stories. They *are* real stories!

DOUBLE BLIND

CAST.
ANDIE: single 28-year-old graduate student
ELAINE: random woman Andie does not
        know but who goes to Andie's
        parents' church
BILL: single 30-year-old guy who, though
        very nice, is nowhere near
        Andie's type

INTERIOR -- CHURCH NARTHEX - DAY

Home from school for the weekend, Andie is attending her parents' new church. After the service, she waits for her mom

and dad in the narthex, a bit uncomfortable as she doesn't know anyone.

> ELAINE
> Hi, Andie! It's sooooooo
> great to see you! How's
> school going?

> ANDIE
> Hi, um. . .

Andie searches her mind for a name, as
she can't remember if she's ever met this
woman.

> ANDIE
> Well, school is going
> great, thanks. . .

> ELAINE
> Are you seeing anyone
> special?

ANDIE

Uh, no, I guess not really,
I uh—

ELAINE

GREAT! Come with me.
Quick!   I've got someone
you need to meet!

Elaine grabs Andie's hand and drags her to
the other side of the narthex where Bill
nervously awaits.

ELAINE

[giddily] Andie, this is Bill.
Bill, this is Andie. I just had
to introduce you since you
have so much in common!
Wonderful! I'll leave you
two alone.

An awkward exchange of small talk ensues
after which Andie excuses herself as
quickly as possible and rushes for cover in
the ladies' room.

Lesson Learned: If you're single too long, people will begin to take all kinds of liberties. If they determine you aren't trying hard enough, they'll take matters into their own hands—even if they have no clue as to who the heck you are.

Guy Talk

Okay, so first of all, you ladies should know that guys get this same stuff—the pressure to meet our mom's best friend's gorgeous niece Lindsey who'll be in town for a weekend on her way back to grad school. And, oh my gosh, Guy and Lindsey just **HAVE** to meet each other. Then they break out the 70 pictures they just happen to have on hand and start in with, "Isn't she stunning! Can you believe she's almost completed her Ph.D. in microbiology? She's only 29!" And I'm thinkin', *Sure, she's hot and all, but she lives halfway across the country and I failed high school bio. This ain't a match, people!*

But no, reason rarely prevails when dealing with middle-aged women and their matchmaking, so of course, the following weekend I find myself on a date with the beautiful and brilliant Lindsey. And yes, she's everything they said she'd be—and I'm smitten.

But here's the kicker—I can tell they had to twist her arm even harder than mine to make this date happen. She's *so* obviously not interested in me or what I'm about and she clearly has way better things than hang out at Applebee's with a biology flunky. And somehow, despite my sincere efforts, she remains unimpressed as I try to regale her with one of my all-time best high school stories—the time when I stuck my dissected frog in my ex-girlfriend's locker. It was awesome—his head was hanging out and everything! She screamed bloody murder and passed out cold in the middle of the hallway. . . (Wow! You're kidding! This story *didn't* impress the lovely Lindsey? — Karin) **Hey, I was trying to connect on the biology thing!** (Right. Good plan. — Karin)

Whatever. So what I'm getting at is—Karin's right. Don't agree to any fix-ups just to appease

125

people. If you're in the mood to give it a shot, go ahead. But if not, take the high road, do the right thing, and give a guy a break. Don't go out on the date in the first place. 'Cause really—and I know I have to keep reminding you—guys have feelings, too.

— Guy

See, this is why we need to hear from the fellas. I couldn't have said it better.

— Karin

Shout Out!

So to my smart, sexy, cream-of-the-crop, A-list, single friends I say this: You aren't screwed up, you don't need another self-help book, and no matter how much people try to tell you otherwise, this isn't a matter of effort. There's nothing more you should or could be doing and nothing you need to change. *"E = MC²"* doesn't translate to

"Effort = Man Catching²". If only finding a guy were as easy as comprehending mass-energy equivalence! It just hasn't happened yet.

Part 2

It Just Hasn't Happened Yet!

a few silly things we

do to ourselves

chapter 7

It Just Hasn't Happened Yet so Stop Thinking About It So Much!

a mind is a terrible thing to waste

A thing I've realized after dating some really-bad-for-me guys is that once we broke up, I was always analyzing myself, trying to figure out what I was doing wrong when, in reality, I was just dating guys that weren't right for me. Now with my current boyfriend I never overanalyze or second-guess myself because he likes me the way I am.

— Katrina, 27

Although women have the reputation of being overly emotional, we're in our heads quite a bit, too. Not that we're necessarily doing anything useful up there. It's often a toss-up between predicting the long-term potential of Bachelor #47 or rehashing the demise of our last five relationships. Or, to be a bit more precise, we're obsessing, ruminating and cogitating about men. And most of the time, it ain't pretty.

Bluntly put, single women think about men—a lot. Many of us spend as much time analyzing guys as we do engaging in other hobbies and interests—especially considering these extracurricular activities often serve as oblique platforms for talking about men anyway.

Even the term *girl talk* is a misnomer and you know it. Who are we kidding? It would be way more appropriate to call it *guy talk*. The topic *du jour* at Sunday brunch? Guys! Discussions over martinis and manicures? Guys! Our weekly phone call to mom? Admit it—guys!

Granted, talking about men is, for most single women, essentially a form of entertainment. But is it really all that fun?

Well, sure, some parts of it are a lot of fun and even serve an essential purpose. Conversation constitutes the foundation of female friendships. It distinguishes us from the testosterone-drenched half of our species. Guys shoot hoops, quail, and shots, whereas chicks chitchat. And true, guys shoot the breeze occasionally, too, but these airy discussions typically center around who's playing center field for the Yankees and not a whole lot more. Women's heart-to-hearts, on the other hand, relay relationship advice, detail dating dilemmas, and bolster break-up bruises and broken hearts. Each feminine exchange solidifies our attachments, deepening their significance.

So though I'm hesitant to censure a revered ritual intrinsic to American womanhood, I submit we might consider better topics to monopolize our neural activity. "Better" because talking about men is hardly a benign pastime. Quite the opposite, it subtly and sneakily demoralizes and demeans us. In all actuality, obsessing about men and overanalyzing our relationships gets us absolutely nowhere and fails to improve our love lives one whit.   And the most damaging part—it keeps us fixated on unavailing cogitation.   We just keep spinning our wheels.

Well, now I sound like a killjoy and maybe just a bit paranoid, too. . .

But hear me out.   We've already discussed the dangers of focusing on that which we can't change (see Chapter 1).   And we've refuted the faulty logic of trying to control the uncontrollable with a self-deprecating method of dreaming up some flaw that, once fixed, will usher in Mr. Right. Not helpful.

Still another problem with thinking too much about guys and rehashing our relationships (or lack thereof) is that it prevents us from appreciating all the fantastic things going on in our lives *now*.   We ignore our good health, our fabulous friends, our stimulating jobs, and our rapidly improving tennis game.   We dismiss all this and exist in limbo, acting as if our lives won't actually begin until we secure a serious relationship.   What a waste of a fab life!

Furthermore, some of us waste not only our fabulous lives but also our fabulous selves. All the appraising, dissecting, and ruminating prompt unwarranted doubts and propel us, at times, to alter who we are. How many times have you and your girlfriends run through the post-date play-by-play, analyzing each conversational exchange and behavioral nuance? Does this sound familiar? "Okay, Clare, here's what happened. We were talking about next weekend and I said I didn't care if we went to his sister's party or not. Then he seemed to get quiet. . . maybe that wasn't the right thing to say. I probably sounded kind of aloof. I bet that's why he hasn't called yet. But I didn't want to look too eager to meet his family. Everyone says you have to play it cool, right? And then when we were talking about the AIDS epidemic in Africa, I kept going on and on about the ONE Campaign. But he didn't have much to say about that, either. He probably got sick and tired of my proselytizing, right? Great, now he thinks I'm totally pushy and opinionated and that I hate his entire family!"

Are you kidding? The guy's reaction likely had absolutely nothing to do with the content of the conversation or his date's opinions. More than likely he just got tired and didn't have anything else to say. Yet she interprets his fatigue and silence as a rejection of core elements of herself—her beliefs and perspectives. And to make matters worse, based on her spurious explanation she begins to adjust her conduct to align with what she incorrectly believes to be her man's preferences. What a racket! And wrong on so many levels! Yet we do it all the time.

Please, if you've got charisma and verve and cogent arguments to articulate, you better keep hopping up on soap boxes and spouting your spiel. It's the essence of who you are and what you're about. Besides, changing for a guy is super lame. And it's a tragic waste of a fabulous mind and a fabulous self.

Psych 101: Why we do it

We're still trapped, really—caught in visceral understandings of our purpose and worth. Women remain excessively concerned with romantic relationships because, for the last few millennia, our very survival depended on snagging and securing a man. And though our existence no longer requires such subjection, we still function within a culture whose gender norms derive from persistent, primordial survival instincts. And unfortunately, these prove almost impossible to shake.

So despite the fact we don't need a man, we want one—bad. And when we don't have one, we feel it—bad.

In addition, our enculturation has done a thorough and exhaustive job leaving us feeling incomplete and inept without a fella. And who wants to feel incomplete and inept? So begins the pondering, obsessing, and ruminating. If we just give it enough deliberation, sufficient brain power, we'll surely figure out which hang-up tanked our last relationship or bring to light any unconscious barriers blocking us from finding a good man in the first place. We're smart women, after all! It can't be all that difficult.

It just hasn't happened yet

Trust me. Analyzing your man and your love life *ad nauseum* gets you nowhere. Strategizing, maneuvering, and gauging prove futile because if your relationship is meant to happen, it will. Frankly, if it's right, you can break every rule, mess up every move, never giving it a second thought, and it'll still work out—because it's right.

Take, for example, my friend, Erica. Erica met Matt at Molly's party. They hit it off right away—joked, laughed, and had a great time. Molly later told Erica that Matt's post-party recap contained a resounding, "Erica rocks!" But Erica didn't hear from Matt. He knew Molly had Erica's number, had already acknowledged an interest in

Erica, yet never bothered to get her number. So Erica called Matt instead. Oops! Mistake #1.

Mistake #2 quickly followed because after a few minutes of chatting on the phone, Erica asked Matt out on a date. That weekend they went out for drinks and dinner and had a fantastic time—so much so that Erica proceeded to Mistake #3—she slept with Matt on the first date.

And did he call the next day? No. So she called him—Mistake #4. Hang tight. It gets better. After six months of dating, Erica suggested Matt move in with her, since he was living in his parents' basement—Mistake #5. A year later, Erica explained to Matt that she was nearing thirty and it would be a good time for him to think about proposing. *All together now*—Mistake #6! So he popped the question. Today Erica and Matt are happily married with three beautiful sons.

Obviously, Erica didn't spend too much time thinking about her game plan. She did it *all* wrong but it turned out *all* right. Because it *was* right.

Ditto

The over-analyzing epidemic has reached a global scale. Apparently, our sisters across the Atlantic possess a similar propensity for excessive scrutinizing of verbal (and digital) exchanges, as evidenced by the musings of British blogger, Natalie Lue:

"We've all been there. Boy meets girl. They have a great time in the honeymoon period, but the girl just has to analyze every phone call, every text, every email and everything that comes out of his mouth. Sometimes I blame technology because the lazy communication that texts and emails yield means that we can interpret stuff whatever way we want to.

Women are supposed to be far more emotional creatures than men and this is great, however we burn up too much brain power obsessing over things that could do with being put on the back burner. Frightening as it may seem, when it comes to male communication, guys either mean what they say/write without any reading between the lines necessary *or* they're lying, end of.

Throw in the fact that guys don't think about the hidden meaning in what they say or write (this is why they apologize very often), which means that if they are being truthful it is a complete waste of time to attempt to read between the lines of a vacant space."

Girl Talk

Karin,

Well, first of all, you're <u>so</u> the pot calling the kettle here. I mean, this entire book is devoted to male/female relationships and how to be cool with yourself till the right guy comes along, etc. But ultimately, it's just one big girl talk, or as you put it— guy talk—session about men!

And really, Karin, women are never gonna stop obsessing about dudes. It's just way too much a part of chick culture. Seriously, what would we have to talk about if we didn't talk about guys?

Now in a way, I agree with you because it's rather ridiculous how we spend hours asking our girlfriends to help us figure out what guys are thinking. But do we ever go straight to the source? No! Then we read all those self-help books claiming to illuminate the male mind, but the catch is the authors are all women. How's that for the blind leading the blind?

But in another way, I don't agree with you. I think we can learn something about men and relationships by talking to our girlfriends. We might figure out things that haven't worked for our girls so we don't make those same mistakes, or we see what a hard time one's having with her man and stay clear of that type of guy. There's got to be some value in it or else we wouldn't do it so much right?

So, I think you should relax a bit and stop raining on our Girl Talk—I mean, Guy Talk—parade!

— Becky, 28

Becky,

Okay. I hear you and I should admit upfront that I felt a little uncomfortable writing this chapter. Clearly, I've spent a ton of time pondering this subject myself—so much so that I wrote a book on it. Yet now I'm trying to tell you to quit obsessing about a topic in which I've immersed myself for the last several years. Hypocrite!

But that's the point. I'm hoping this book will help us *all* to stop thinking about our man-less status so much—or at least think about it differently.

I'm hoping we'll begin to catch ourselves when we slip up—those times when we think, "Maybe there is something wrong with me. . ." And that we'll resist buying into society's "marriage-at-all-costs" mandate and check our faulty cognition and skewed reasoning, i.e. *if I just do _____, he'll show up!* Squandered genius! Frittered brilliance! No more desecrating precious neural energy on trivialities!

I know, I know. I'm hopping off the soapbox now.

— Karin

The Awful Truth

Remember, these scenes are not *based* on real stories. They *are* real stories!

OBSESSIVE COMPULSIVE DISASTER

CAST.
MEGHAN: 35-year-old corporate attorney
HILLARY: her new coworker, who just
started at the firm

INTERIOR -- DOWNTOWN BAR - NIGHT

It's Friday evening and the women are enjoying an after-work cocktail. They've just recently met and are getting to know each other, as women often do, by talking about their love lives. Meghan has been prattling on about a failed relationship for the past 20 minutes.

MEGHAN

. . . so as for Jimmy, I've
never really been able to
figure out why we only
made it a few months—
although my friend Dana
said it was because I was
putting closure on my
relationship with my last
boyfriend, Corey, by
trying to "work it out"
with my next boyfriend.
And since Jimmy was the
next guy I dated after
Corey, I ended up
dragging along all my
Corey-baggage, you know
what I mean? Almost like
how girls with absentee
dads will keep dating guys
who can't commit because
it's like if they can get
some guy to stick around
it will somehow make up
for the fact that their

144

dads were never there for them. But I don't know if that's really what I was doing, but that was Dana's take on it, you know?

HILLARY

Wow. It sounds like that relationship really did a number on you.

MEGHAN

Oh yeah, for sure.

HILLARY

How serious were you? Were you talking marriage?

MEGHAN

Oh, my gosh, no! Jimmy and I dated during my junior year in high school!

145

Lesson Learned: We can waste a lot of time and energy psychoanalyzing ancient history. Don't we have anything better to do? As long as we're consumed by the past, we fail to step into our bright future! Let's get to it!

Guy Talk

Wow. This chapter is a real window into Chick World. So you women just talk about men all day, every day? Man, I wish I'd known this little gem a long time ago. But at the same time, when it comes to this subject, it's funny, because in a way we're really not all that different. True, on a given Sunday afternoon, guys are talking smack while playing pick-up basketball, not complaining about their lady troubles over brunch. But trust me, the sports are just a cover up. Guys obsess about women plenty. We just don't 'fess up to it as much—definitely not to each other and maybe not even to ourselves.

And I'm not saying that our way is the healthiest approach either, but guys are in a rough spot with this stuff. Society dictates confining expectations for men, too you know. I mean, we're supposed to be tough and hard—a "man's man"—and if we show any weakness or sensitivity we're considered pansies or sissies. So, we're not too apt to start crying in our beer when we're out with the boys or even when we're out with you. Because, although you women say you want us to communicate and express our emotions, sometimes it bites us in the butt.

Take, for example, my friend Jay. He dated Renée for about six months, during which time she constantly pined for her ex-boyfriend, a rugged, tough-guy construction worker from New Zealand. Jay, a writer and musician, is a more artistic guy and initially Renée loved his sensitivity—especially as he played therapist trying to repair her broken heart. But eventually the novelty of his "emo" vibe wore off and Renée started making cracks about his sexuality. When he wore a turtle neck sweater, she called him "femmy". When he couldn't figure out how to put wheel covers on her car, she ridiculed. When he flubbed up the assembly of her new Ikea bookcase. . . well what kind of man was he anyway? All this plus an incessant need to talk about their relationship? He had to be gay!

And you know how sexy it makes a guy feel when his girlfriend accuses him of being gay. Yeah, they didn't last too long after that.

But back to the point. We think a lot about women, too. We might not talk about it—because, as Jay's situation pointed out, that can backfire—but we think about you.

— Guy

Well, it feels good to know men obsess about us sometimes as well. And from the way Guy puts it, they have it worse because at least chick culture permits us to dish about men and talk about our feelings without having anyone question our sexuality. See, we women can be horrible about this stuff! We beg and plead guys to "open up" and share what they're feeling. Then when they do, we hit 'em with the "don't be such a wuss!" bit. Not nice, ladies. Not nice at all.

— Karin

Shout Out!

So to my smart, sexy, cream-of-the-crop, A-list, single friends I say this: You aren't screwed up, you don't need another self-help book, and no matter how much you analyze and ruminate, the whole deal is out of your control anyway. You're great women and you didn't mess anything up. There's nothing more you should or could be doing and nothing you need to change. Let's find new subject matter for Girl Talk and give our armchair psychologists a break. Besides, a mind is a terrible thing to waste—especially one as whip smart as yours! It just hasn't happened yet.

chapter 8

It Just Hasn't Happened Yet so Don't Compare Yourself to Your Married Friends!

keeping up with the Joans

My friends used to tell me stuff like this when we were younger and they were married. And I kept thinking something was wrong because I didn't have someone in my life. Then I met my guy and I've been with him for 5 years (I <u>was</u> picky, by the way—we should be). But what's interesting is my friends are now either divorced or really dissatisfied with their marriages. All that time I felt I was missing out on being in love and being married and now they're <u>not</u> happy and they want to be single again!

— Mandy, 42

Comparison games. They're not just played by suburban couples trying to "keep up with the Joneses". We women compete in a Powder Puff League of this sport—"Keeping Up with the *Joans*". And the longer you stay single, the lower you rank, since you have yet to score the only point that matters in this match—marriage.

But your friends have much better luck. One by one they hit grand slams, skip around the bases, and march toward the home-plate altar, which, interestingly, alters the delicate dynamics of your relationships. That lovely day in June granted her more than a new name and a bit of left-hand bling. It also garnered her a measure of social credibility and respect reserved solely for women bearing the title of "Mrs.". Friends who were once on your level advance and become your superiors. The balance tips and it's disconcerting. Some women lord it over you, *à la* "Things are so different for me now—you'll understand once you're married." Most don't. Nevertheless, you feel it. In society's eyes, and maybe in each other's eyes, you're no longer the same.

You wonder how it all happened, anyway. *What did Joan do to land a CEO while I'm still meeting BOZOs! Seriously? I dated way more guys than she did in college! Besides, she's not as pretty as I am! And she's such a complainer. Plus, she's got ugly feet. Has Mark seen her in sandals?*

Annoyed by your own pettiness, you check yourself. *What's my problem? What's with all this catty jealousy? Besides, I'm totally happy for her! I don't begrudge her a bit. After all, she's one of my best friends.*

Still, you marvel at how love's been so easy for her yet so tough for you. In an attempt to discern the secret of her success, you take stock of what she has to offer versus what you bring to the table. And that's all it takes. Just like that, without even realizing it, you've started a round of "Keeping Up with the Joans".

See how easy it is to slip into that way of thinking? You're not catty! You're not envious of your friends! You can't believe you got sucked into playing silly comparison games in the first place. But you did. And absolutely no good will come of it.

Because a round of "Keeping Up with the Joans" proves infuriating for two reasons. First of all, you're irritated with yourself for making parallels because it's trifling and lame and you know it.

But perhaps even more maddening is you can't really pinpoint where you fall short. In fact, you think you measure up pretty well to your friend, yet your girl's the one who nabbed a man. Hmmm. How'd that happen?

Let me take a stab at it—and I'm not trying to be harsh, I'm really not, but this book is meant to encourage single women, so I'm worried about *your* feelings, not the feelings of your happily married friends. So I'm just going to be frank here for a minute.

It's not that I want to put anyone down, but the point is, and you know this if you're honest with yourself, you are *way* cooler than a lot of your married friends. And as for their husbands? Please, you know you wouldn't have gone on even one date with most of them! So why are you so jealous? Because you got caught up in comparisons, that's why!

Plus, when playing "Keeping Up with the Joans", you inadvertently subscribe to the bogus logic that since you're still single, you're losing the competition and are therefore off your game. Right. As if that makes any sense! So the average 35-year-old married woman is superior to the average 35-year-old single woman? The wife has fewer emotional hang-ups than her single counterpart just because she's married? Or she's more talented and has a better personality? Seriously? Where's the sense in that? Half of your married friends settled anyway, and you know it. I mean, if anyone's got issues, they do! But no one sees it that way. It's as if once a woman marries, she's *arrived* and even if she has to spend the rest of her life with a complete tool, it doesn't matter, because at least she's *married*. And we all buy into it. When actually, you took the harder path and didn't settle for a dork like some of your friends did! (Okay, that was a little harsh—sorry!)

The tragedy lies in the fact that we minimize, or completely ignore, the courageous decision we've made to wait for the right person. Instead of seeing ourselves as gutsy and self-sufficient in our singleness, we insist we possess myriad weaknesses. Come on! It's exactly the opposite! We singles risk being alone forever, refusing to resign ourselves to a mediocre relationship. That's pretty brave and impressive. We enjoy our *own* company on weekend nights. We handle our *own* bank accounts and pull up our *own* Mapquests. We cheer on our *own* careers and dry our *own* tears. But instead of giving ourselves our *own* "high fives", we search for imperfections and scramble to bookstores to identify the *Ten Stupid Things You Do to Chase Away Mr. Right* or *Mistakes Women Make After 30 That Keep Them from Walking Down the Aisle.* We downplay the chancy, courageous choice we've made while elevating the easy, wussy choice made by some of our friends. Do you see what we do to ourselves?

Granted, not all your friends settled. And a few of them have great husbands—smart, funny, accomplished guys—the type you'd like to end up with. Well, I've got a newsflash for you. I *know* the secret to their success and I'm here to reveal this highly sensitive, classified information. Are you ready? Brace yourself. *THEY GOT LUCKY!* Yep, you heard me. It was just plain luck. They happened to meet an amazing guy in freshman English and were able to avoid all the angst and uncertainty of independent, single adulthood. Pure luck. But that's not how we perceive it. We compare ourselves to our friends, strike up a round of "Keeping Up with the Joans", and assume the wives did something right while we keep messing up.

Psych 101: Why we do it

Why do we judge ourselves against our friends? Why insist we're flawed? Why minimize our gutsy choice?

Let's start with society and I know I keep pointing the finger at this nebulous "society" thing, but, truly, society is guilty in this case with its simple formula of *"Married = Good / Single = Bad"*. Our culture conceptualizes singles as overgrown children trapped in adult bodies, selfishly wasting away our days in irresponsible laziness and frivolity. Meanwhile, married people contribute responsibly and generously to all factions of civilization in an industrious, committed, and mature manner.

I wish I'd made up such impressions for effect, but unfortunately, research backs these assessments. Since we're taking Psych 101 here and not a grad course I'll leave out the details, but studies find most people, married and unmarried alike, view singles in a much more negative light than those who are married. Meaning, even we singles look down on each other and ourselves.

This mentality sneaks into countless elements of our daily existence and sometimes, no matter how strong we are, we get exhausted. Weary of fending off the *"Single = Bad"* formula, we give in. *If I compare myself to Joan maybe I can figure it all out—what she's got that I don't, what she's doing right that I'm doing wrong. I'm tired of being inferior. For once, I want to win this game.*

It just hasn't happened yet

Okay, I admit it. In supporting my single girls, I played some comparison games myself. I pitted you against your married friends, suggesting they sold out and you didn't. I compared their wimpy choice to your courageous one. I insinuated they didn't have the guts to go it alone, so they caved and coupled.

Am I sorry? Nope. Again, I wasn't trying to rip on your married friends. That's not the point. But single women take hits all the time. People offend us at every turn with their insensitive appraisals and irrational perspectives. Prevailing societal conceptions accuse us of insufficiency and ineptitude. We unwittingly internalize such judgments and then do battle with the voices in our heads telling us we're disturbed, damaged, and doomed.

So, this chapter brought you a different message: one about how cool, gutsy, and fabulous we actually are!

Ditto

Maybe we wouldn't try so hard to keep up with the Joans if singles were accorded the same respect as other adults—if the assessment of our worth reflected our contribution to society, as opposed to our marital status. And just to set the record straight here and now, according to the research of Dr. Bella DePaulo, author of *Singled Out: How Singles are Stereotyped, Stigmatized, and Ignored and Still Live Happily Ever After,* single adults are typically more generous with charitable contributions and acts of service to the community than married adults.

Nevertheless, pejorative perceptions remain, as noted by Miriam Greenwald of UnmarriedAmerica.org:

"Not all married people are mature or wise... Why is even the most dysfunctional couple elevated above the best adjusted single person? Because according to society the very fact of being perpetually single brings into question everything else. Or if you are truly alone, how, according to others, can you by definition be well adjusted? Since only the credentials of marriage attest to 'normal' adjustment!"

Girl Talk

Karin,

You nailed me in this chapter. You basically told my exact story. Not to sound like I'm bragging, but in college, I was "it"! I was president of my sorority, fraternity sweetheart four years in a row, and as for guys? Please, I think I spent maybe two weekends alone during my entire college career. I mean, it was so easy then. I'd break up with one boyfriend and meet another in the caf the very next day! Done and done! And again, I'm not trying to blow my own horn, but really, I went out with way more guys than any of my friends.

But check this out. My roommate, Alyssa, well, she didn't go out with anyone from freshman to junior year. Maybe a date here and there, but nothing serious at all. I don't think she went to even one Homecoming. Then all of a sudden she meets this guy, Rob, in a senior seminar and BAM! It's over. They dated for three years, moved to Portland together, and now they're about to buy a condo in the Pearl district. Oh, and did I mention the ROCK on her left hand? Yeah, it's gotta be three carats.

And I love Alyssa and all, but how did she hit the jackpot and I'm still going out with crack pots?

— Holly, 27

Holly,

Your story just proves my point. All those years in college, you're out with a different guy every night while Alyssa's back in the dorm room knitting socks and baking cookies. You know she's a great girl, but she's not turning too many heads. Until that one day it happens—connection! She meets him and, as you put it, it's over. Of course, you know Alyssa's not prettier than you or smarter than you or funnier than you. And she's certainly no more emotionally stable or less neurotic than you just because she happened to run into Rob in senior seminar. She's not a better "catch" than you. She just met her match and you haven't yet. Simple as that.

Oh, and you didn't mention it, which was gracious of you, but I'm betting that although from time to time you feel jealous of their relationship, you probably wouldn't want to marry a guy like Rob anyway. Am I right? 'Cause really, if you could have been happy with a "Rob" type, you probably would have met an equivalent version of him in *your* senior seminar. Don't you think?

— Karin

The Awful Truth

Remember, these scenes are not *based* on real stories. They *are* real stories!

HEY JEALOUSY

CAST.
RACHEL: 26-year-old kindergarten teacher
EMILY: Rachel's friend

INTERIOR -- WINE BAR - NIGHT

EMILY
So how was Frannie's wedding? Wasn't it last weekend?

163

RACHEL

Oh my gosh! It was
fantastic! Her folks must
have dropped at least 100
grand. So snazzy! So
fun!

EMILY

That's great. I love a
high-end wedding!
Yummy food, cool band,
you get to dance all
night...

RACHEL

For sure. But get this—
when she was walking
down the aisle, Frannie
tripped! It was horrible!
I was so embarrassed for
her!

EMILY

Oh, no! That's the worst!

RACHEL

I know, it was really bad.
But just between us, I was
kinda glad it happened.
Just a little bit.

EMILY

Huh?

RACHEL

Well, I mean, I'm not
trying to be a horrible
person, but you know
how it is—there I was,
"always the bridesmaid,
never the bride", and
Frannie's there with her
perfect groom and her
perfect dress and her
perfect wedding and you
know, I was kinda glad
that her tripping down
the aisle made it—well,
not perfect.

EMILY

Wow, with best friends
like you, who needs
enemies?

RACHEL

What are you trying to
say?

EMILY

Well, I guess her wedding
truly was a fairy tale,
wasn't it? Complete with
a wicked step-sister
bridesmaid!

Lesson Learned: The jealousy that consumes us
when we indulge in comparison games is super-
unattractive and, as Emily pointed out, hardly the
way friends should act toward one another. And
we're just way too fabulous for that!

Guy Talk

Okay, I'm sorry, but this chapter was kinda hilarious for me! Aren't aggression and competitiveness supposed to be linked to testosterone? What's wrong with you women? All the catfighting and carrying on. . .

Maybe I just don't get it because guys don't think this way. Certainly not when it comes to being married, anyway—we usually get dragged down the aisle kicking and screaming, right? So we don't see our friends as superior to us just because we haven't found ourselves a wife.

Maybe we lack the jealousy gene or something. Because we definitely don't go for the jugular the way women do. It's like, if my buddy shows up to a party with some gorgeous woman I think, "What's up with that? If that joker can do it so can I! I gotta get me a hottie, too." But I don't seethe about it and hold it against him and get mad because I dated more cheerleaders than he did in high school.

No offense, Karin. But this is really a nasty window into chick culture.

— Guy

Wait a minute, so you're trying to tell me guys don't get jealous of each other? Are you kidding? What with all the posturing and chest thumping and cruising around in hot rods with silicone-enhanced candy on each arm. Come on, Guy.

I think I see your point, though. But it all goes back to how we're evaluated. A woman's worth is determined by her relationships, while a man's net-worth determines his value. So with men, we might see a little more cut-throat activity in the business realm, whereas with women, the backstabbing occurs in the social milieu. Come to think of it, have you ever been to a trading floor? I rest my case.

— Karin

Shout Out!

So to my smart, sexy, cream-of-the-crop, A-list, single friends I say this: You aren't screwed up, you don't need another self-help book, and no matter how much you compare yourselves to your married friends, you'll never figure out what they did "right" and you did "wrong". They aren't any better or worse than you. They aren't any more or less messed up. They got lucky. And one of these days, you will, too. There's nothing more you should or could be doing and nothing you need to change. Please—no more "Keeping Up with the Joans". You, kitten, are way too cool to play that catty game. It just hasn't happened yet.

chapter 9

It Just Hasn't Happened Yet so Take a Break from Online Dating!

it's just a singles' bar in cyberspace

It's like I feel this pressure to be online all the time. Like the man of my dreams could be a mouse click away and what if I miss him because I let my FindTheOne.com subscription expire?

— Carla, 37

And yes, I know your friend, Chrissy, met the love of her life online. Okay. So that makes one. Can you name anyone else who did? How many of your friends have tried it? Or should I ask, how many have been successful? Better question—of the individuals your friends *have* met online, what caliber of gentlemen are we talking about? Would *you* consider going out with these guys? Be honest. See, that's my point.

It's not that dating sites never work. Occasionally they do the trick. With the huge number of people putting up profiles nowadays, eventually some get lucky. Which, of course, proves annoying for the rest of us because their success provides platitudinal ammo for those on the outside—i.e., another way for people to claim we're doing something wrong which is why we're single: "But you haven't even given eHusband.com a chance! You said yourself that Chrissy met her fiancé on that site!"

So after getting reamed enough, you figure you better at least try it. It can't hurt anything and it's got to increase your odds of finding a boyfriend, right? Not necessarily.

Think about it. If you walked into a coworker's cocktail party on any given Saturday night, no matter how many guys showed up, you'd likely find yourself attracted to only a certain portion of them. Let's say roughly 20% of the fellas would pique your interest, with the other 80% leaving you completely flat. Naturally, of the ones you deemed appealing, half would drive you nuts the minute they opened their mouth—unless, of course, these guys bore a resemblance to Jude Law, in which case you'd put up with innumerable asinine utterances just to bask in their physical perfection for a while. But barring that potentiality, you're left with a possible connection with roughly one out of every ten guys. Put those percentages to work on LoveOfYourLife.com and you'll see what you're dealing with. Loads of men. No increase, however, in the proportion of those with prospective compatibility.

But since there are more men online than at your coworker's cocktail party, if we're talking sheer numbers, we definitely increase our chances of success by trying the websites, right? Not necessarily, and here's why. If the population of gentlemen cruising around online is representative of the population of gentlemen at your coworker's cocktail party, then, yes, you'll have a probable connection with roughly 10% of them. But if the online population doesn't mirror the demographic of your coworker's party, then, sadly, that percentage will probably be less. In fact, one might argue that devoting too much time to finding a boyfriend online potentially *decreases* your odds of finding a partner.

Why? Because the online thing is a complete free-for-all! At least when run into a prospect while going about your business, you have a reasonable chance of having one or two things in common. The very fact that you happened upon each other while living your typical day in your typical world suggests some promise. If you bump into a cute guy at your favorite restaurant, you apparently have similar tastes in cuisine. Or if you strike up a conversation with a fellow attendee at a professional conference, you clearly work in similar industries. Or if your introduction occurs at a dinner party, you share mutual friends and travel in similar circles. But if you meet someone online, it's possible that the only thing you have in common is your ability to enter a URL address—which might not get you very far once the relationship begins.

Another reason your odds have *not* increased involves the anonymity of cyberspace. Okay, how can I put this delicately? Let's go back to the men from your coworker's cocktail party. Remember the 80% you found unattractive? Well, in a real-life situation, although some of those fellows might be interested in you, most of them would readily pick up your vibe of disinterest and leave you alone. Admittedly, a few clueless characters would cruise over armed with a drink and a bad pickup line, but the majority would recognize they didn't have a chance, at least not until they'd garnered some liquid courage.

Not so in cyberworld. Again, I'm trying to be sensitive here, but if you post a profile online, you're going to get hits from guys who would *never ever* have the nerve to approach you in a bar or dance club. Not in a million years! But that cyberdistance gives all kinds of men all kinds of guts.

Psych 101: Why we do it

We do it for any number of reasons. Perhaps friends have badgered us into trying harder (see Chapter 6) but instead of rustling up a blind date, they hopped online and put together a profile for us on Mismatch.com, and we indulge them in order to get them off our backs. Or maybe this week's water-cooler gossip consisted of a slew of online dating fairy tales and you got caught up in the hype. Of course, the television commercials could have caught your eye; they can be pretty persuasive on a solitary Saturday night. Or then again, you could have just been really bored.

It just hasn't happened yet

Which, by the way, is what you'll need to be—very, very bored—because online dating takes up a *lot* of time! First off, you'll spend hours trying to write the perfect biographical sketch, certain your entire future rests in this profile's packaging so it better be good! You'll want to come across as cute, but not cutesy. Funny, but not wacky. Intelligent, but not nerdy. Composing the document will take a minimum of six or seven hours, after which you'll force all your girlfriends to preview and edit it before you go live. An utter waste of time, by the way, since no man in the history of online dating has read even a single word of a woman's profile. Please—they go straight for the pictures.

Which leads to the next time-consuming operation: selecting your photos—more painful and arduous decisions! You want to look beautiful, but not stuck up. Professional, but not stiff. Sexy, but not slutty. Though horribly laborious, at least the hours consumed by this activity pay off since your pictures will be carefully and repeatedly scrutinized by several thousand men in cyberland—a somewhat disconcerting concept in and of itself, if you stop to think about it.

And finally, after completing your profile, you'll take a turn perusing what the gentlemen have to offer. Contrary to the fantastical contemplations of your married friends, this exercise bears absolutely no resemblance to kids frolicking in candy stores. In fact, the whole tortuous ordeal typically drains and discourages you further as you click through umpteen million profiles of dudes saying the exact same thing:

- I'm a [**insert:** middle management position] at [your town's big firm or business].

- I love going to [**insert:** random indie band you've never heard of] shows.

- I'm the HUGEST [**insert:** your city's major league baseball team] fan ever!

- I love moonlit walks on the beach
[**insert:** Liar!].

Mind you, all of the above give you no useful information whatsoever because it describes *every single man* between the ages of 21 and 71. They might as well have written that they breathe on a regular basis and rely on food to nourish their bodies. Furthermore, as evidenced by the bit about loving moonlit walks on the beach, cyberdistance encourages truth stretching in myriad ways. . .

So you scroll and scroll and troll and troll and as your eyes glaze over you feel increasingly bored and hopeless. But the worst part? On top of the apathy and *ennui*, you also feel mean, cruel, and harsh. Why? Because pulling up a profile, awakens your inner critic—*Oh, I don't think so! Please! He calls that an athletic build?* and *Are you kidding me? There is no way this dude is 32!* or *This guy is so not cute to me! And neither is he. . . and neither is he. . . and neither is he. . .* More often than not, you end up more disheartened than before you got online. You start wondering if the two hours per night you devote to perusing profiles would be much better spent snuggled up in bed with a cat and a good book.

Earlier in the chapter I said it couldn't hurt anything to do a little online dating. Yeah, well I take it all back.

Ditto

We've been trying this stuff forever, you know. Before matchmaking websites entered the scene, video services and personal ads provided avenues for single women to meet men. But these techniques bore the same inherent drawbacks as online dating:

"The goal—intimacy—is about the whole person: her context, her work, her friends, her family, the life she has constructed, her interests, the way she listens, the way she shares, how much she has to offer, and how much she wants to take. The process—services such as video dating and personal ads—removes her from her context and draws attention only to what she has to show—her

face, her figure, her ability to say something pithy
in two minutes on tape or 45 minutes over coffee."
— Lee Reilly, *Women Living Single: Thirty
Women Share Their Stories of Navigating
Through a Married World*

Girl Talk

Karin,

> *I am done with online dating. Done and done!
> I'm sick of it! I hate it! It just makes me feel like crap!*
>
> *And here's exactly why: I had a date last
> Sunday night with a guy I met online. He was okay
> looking, but soooooooooo boring. All he talked about for
> two straight hours was fantasy football and golf! Um,
> do I look like I care about either one of those things?
> But of course, I'm nice as pie during dinner, laughing,
> smiling "Wow, that's fascinating! Blah, blah, blah. . .
> lie, lie, lie." So then we're wrapping things up and
> getting ready to leave and he goes, "Have a nice
> Thanksgiving. Good luck." And I'm thinking, "Are*

you kidding me? You're not going to call <u>me</u>?!? You're dissing <u>me</u> after I put up with your monologue on driving irons and dynasty leagues?!? Well then, screw you, Mr. I-am-so-boring-I-make-my-dates-want-to-poke-their-eyes-out-with-a-fork!"

I'm so sick and tired of being rejected. I know I shouldn't feel this way, but I do. And everyone's like, "Just go online!" Well, actually I hate to break it to them, but going online does absolutely nothing but make me feel bad. Either I have horrible dates like this one or the guys I'm actually interested in email me for weeks but never call! At this point even if I'm not all that interested, it would be nice for SOMEONE to call. No, I should take that back. I did have one guy call, but unfortunately, he was utterly nuts!

I feel like I'm in such a bad place with all this, but how else am I supposed to feel? I can't even find Mr. Meantime, never mind Mr. Right!

Sorry to rant and rave, I'm just a little frustrated. I quit GetMarried.com and I'm for sure done with Connect.com. I've decided to chuck it all and keep focusing on myself.

I've tossed around the idea of joining "Lunch Date to Find a Mate" but right now, I don't have the *energy for it. I'm so defeated by this online business, I got nothin' left.*

— Whitney, 35

Whitney,

Thanks for your candor and I'm sure it wasn't easy given how cruddy you're feeling right now. Trust me, the single women reading your letter are totally empathizing with you; we've all been there at one point or another.

One thing you mentioned really stood out to me—how everyone tells you, "Just go online!" It's another one of the infuriating comments people are forever throwing our way. Clearly, most of them have never had to pursue the awkwardness of Internet dating because if they had, they'd realize there's no "just" about it. It's a highly laborious and involved activity, not to mention possibly expensive.

And your rotten experience gives a perfect example of how risky and painful online dating can be. You can really get punched in the gut and feel completely rejected by guys you didn't even find attractive in the first place! Still, that rejection stings. . . Great. You've been feeling lonely for a while, and now you get to feel lonely *and* rejected. Wow! What a great experience this "just go online" thing turned out to be! Thanks for the fantastic advice, everybody!

— Karin

The Awful Truth

Remember, these scenes are not *based* on real stories. They *are* real stories!

EHOMELY.COM

CAST.
ANNETTE: 36-year-old single, HR manager
RITA: Dating Website Customer Service
Representative

INTERIOR -- ANNETTE'S APARTMENT - DAY

Annette is on the phone with Rita, a customer service representative of a popular dating website.

> RITA
> Thank you for calling
> eHomely Customer Care.
> This is Rita.

> ANNETTE
> Hi, Rita. I've got a few
> concerns with my
> eHomely membership.
> I've been with the
> program for two months
> now and, frankly, I find
> this service to be very
> unsuccessful in finding
> me a match. I've
> communicated with
> several men up until the
> e-mailing process and

then they fail to follow through. I've nudged them, as stated in your website's recommendations, but still nothing. Could you please explain how I go about getting a refund?

RITA

Annette, we appreciate your concern about not receiving any matches and we're here to offer you assistance. First, I'd like to highly recommend that you consider retaking the Relationship Questionnaire. We have six psychologists constantly researching and updating the Questionnaire and we're confident that upon retaking it, your ability to

be matched will be that
much greater.

ANNETTE
No, thank you, Rita. I'm
not interested in retaking
the questionnaire. I put a
significant amount of time
and thought into the
questions the first time. I
highly doubt my core
opinions and values have
changed dramatically in
the past two months.

RITA
That's understandable,
Annette. May I make
another suggestion? As
you have already nudged
your matches, I
recommend you close
communication with those
who have not yet
responded to your efforts

by providing the reason
"This match never
responded to my request
to communicate."

ANNETTE
Thanks for the tip, Rita,
but I always close the
matches after I nudge
them and they don't
respond. By the way, the
"nudge" option, in my
opinion, is not helpful. I
have not yet had anyone
respond to the "nudge".
It's humiliating to have to
nudge anyway, which
basically translates to
"I'm desperate and need
your attention." Maybe
the men just don't have
the energy to hit the
"close" button. If that's
the case, I'd rather not

date someone as lazy as
this anyway.

RITA

Okay. Well then, that's
not the problem. May I
share another suggestion
that may prove
successful? Posting
photos is a great way to
engage your matches and
get conversations flowing.
I see that you already
have six great pictures,
and I would encourage
you to consider adding as
many as possible. This
can truly help your match
understand the many
aspects of your
personality and lifestyle,
those qualities that make
you who you are.

ANNETTE

Honestly, Rita, I feel six
photos is quite appropri-
ate. My pictures are
current and show me in a
variety of settings. Is
this a dog-and-pony show
or a dating site? Not to
mention the fact that
most of the men's
pictures look more like
mug shots from jail!
Some of the guys actually
take self-portraits in their
bathroom mirrors.
Personally, I'd prefer not
to date someone who uses
a camera in the
bathroom. Besides, a lot
of the men post no
pictures at all. But I'm
supposed to put up 27?

RITA

Annette, I hear your
concerns and I'm sorry
you've not been success-
ful so far. I'd like to ask
you to reconsider taking
to heart some of the
suggestions I mentioned.

ANNETTE

So basically you're telling
me that somehow it's my
fault these men aren't
interested in me or that
my profile is not eye-
catching enough. Thanks
a lot. You know, it seems
like the pervasive view of
single women is "What
are they doing wrong?
Why can't they get a
man?" Does anyone
consider how much time
and effort we invest in
finding a partner?

Blaming a single woman
assumes there's
something wrong with
her. That's a pretty sad
viewpoint—especially for
a dating website.
Actually Rita, I'm tired of
talking about this and
clearly you're reading off
some sort of script so
we're not getting
anywhere at all. May I
please just have my
refund?

RITA
Again, Annette, I'd like to
reiterate that I hear your
concerns but I regret that
we cannot process your
request for a refund.
Please be aware that
early termination of your
account does not result in
a prorated refund. After

the trial period has
expired, we require that
you stay the entire length
of your subscription.

            ANNETTE
Rita, your policy is
ridiculous! This is a
"service" you provide
and if the service is not
given, a refund should be
issued!

Rita pauses.

            RITA
Thank you for calling,
Annette. The good news
is, we have 15,000 new
users registering every
day. We're confident
we'll help you find the
love of your life.

Lesson learned: Online dating is a business. We forget that because the industry involves our love lives, but it's still a for-profit venture, ladies. Simply put, they want your money. The next time someone tells you to "just go online" let them read this little exchange. Maybe they'll get the picture.

Guy Talk

Let me take a minute to defend my half of the species because I'm not sure what's up with some of Karin's rhetoric here. For one, not all men lie on their online profiles (as Karin insinuated) and some guys don't like baseball (although I don't personally know any and they probably have part of their Y chromosome missing) and some of us truly do like walks on the beach (especially if there's the chance of a moonlight skinny dip). C'mon, Anderson! What's with all the sexist statements?

I do have to agree with Karin, though, that the online thing can be a shot in the dark. But it's like that for guys, too. Women misrepresent themselves in their profiles just as often as men do. Sometimes your date shows up and you know for a fact her profile picture was taken a minimum of 10 years and 40 pounds ago. Or one time, I went out with a woman who, after a drink or two, made it quite clear she was in the market for a corporate type making high six figures. I was thinking, "Did this gold-digger somehow miss that I'm a writer and I checked the $20,000 – $40,000 income box?"

So I get why you're frustrated at times, but then again, it doesn't hurt to try, right? (I take it you didn't actually read the whole chapter then, Guy. I made it clear that sometimes it *does* hurt to try! — Karin)

Oh yeah, my bad. I forgot how painful it is for you women. When you're ripping these guys' profiles to shreds and lamenting that none of them are good enough for you, it makes you feel like a big, fat meany (actually, I've got another word for it, but. . .) Yeah, that's rough, ladies, because who wants to feel judgmental and harsh when you're really being, well— judgmental and harsh! "Woe is me! I'm too perfect for any of these mooks, and it's so hurtful to realize it!" Nice.

All I'm saying is give us a break every once in a while! Go out with the dude whose picture is a little goofy because he's not the most photogenic person alive or hold back on writing a guy off just because he has yet to acquire vacation property. A lot of these fellas are shy and nervous and it's gonna show up on their profile. Give 'em a chance to show up in person and make a case for themselves.

— Guy

Well then. I'm not going to even dignify certain elements of the preceding statement by attempting to defend my position. I'll simply reiterate that online dating *is* risky and *can* hurt both parties involved. Guys ridicule our profiles, too, and we get rejected, as well (see Whitney's letter). But, as I always say, I asked for a guy's opinion so. . . Be careful what you ask for; you just might get it.

— Karin

Shout Out!

So to my smart, sexy, cream-of-the-crop, A-list, single friends I say this: You aren't screwed up, you don't need another self-help book, and going online won't guarantee you'll meet the love of your life any easier or any sooner. You're great women and there's nothing more you should or could be doing and nothing you need to change. Don't let the sappy commercials and slick advertising suck you in. Can't buy me love! It just hasn't happened yet.

chapter 10

It Just Hasn't Happened Yet so Don't Get Back Together with Your Ex-Boyfriend!
the definition of insanity. . .

Tonight was a gem. First, I made plans to have dinner with an ex. Smart. Then, I was feeling girlie and frisky and decided to text a different ex, to ask him if he wanted to make out. Seriously, who does that? Apparently I do. His response was that he didn't think it would be a good idea and that we should probably discuss it later. I told him there's nothing to discuss, I'm just looking for fun. Just making out, no strings attached. There's a reason why we didn't work out, no need to rehash that. Now we have plans to watch TV on Thursday night. Obviously, I just never quite understand the concept that ex-boyfriends are ex-boyfriends for a reason.

— Nina, 25

I've been there. You've been there. We've all been there—especially if you've been single for a while. You haven't had a date in months—haven't laid eyes on anyone you find even remotely attractive. This toxic cocktail of three-parts nasty dry spell and one-part penchant for glorifying the past leaves you extremely vulnerable to your ex-boyfriend's "Let's give it one more try" proposition. Bam! Before you know it, you're back in the fray—the ex-fray.

Of course, you have your reasons. Some of which are halfway legit. Maybe you live in a small town with a shallow pool of eligible bachelors or you tend to have a hard time working your ex-boyfriends out of your system or you're just flat out lonely. Whatever the explanation, the outcome remains the same—a revolving-door approach to relationships that keeps you in an on-again/off-again holding pattern.

You've heard the definition of insanity, right? "Doing the same thing over and over and expecting different results." Interestingly, both Ben Franklin and Albert Einstein receive credit for coining the maxim. I would have sworn the quote came from a single woman burned repeatedly by forays into the ex-fray.

One more quote for you: "As a dog that returns to his vomit, so is a fool who repeats his folly." Sorry about the vulgar imagery, but I'm trying to make a point. And at some level you know it—because though you try to convince yourself it'll be different this time, you can't completely stifle the little voice inside asking, *if we didn't work out before, what do we have going for us now*? Will the second (or third or fourth) time be the charm? Really? How?

Naturally, as a veteran girl-about-town, you've likely been on both sides of this story. You've broken up with boyfriends, but then panicked and begged them back within the week. Next time around you got the heave-ho, but a month later answered the phone to a "My bad! Can we try it again?" And sure, we're drawn to the romantic notion that stars might uncross and stabilize a previously shaky relationship, but do we *really* believe it?

Furthermore, let's look at the cold, hard facts. I hate to be the one to remind you, but if your ex did the breaking up, he decided to *improve* his life by *removing* you. Remember that. Keep it prominent in your mind. He had you and let you go. He risked never laying eyes on you again. Period. So what's his explanation for wanting you back so bad now? Did the girl he dumped you for return the favor? Has he decided to quit searching for the love of his life and settle for you? That sounds promising.

Similarly, if you broke up with him, you need to recall the circumstances that incited your exit and consider any underlying motivations for reuniting. Do you truly want him back or are you just tired of dateless Saturday nights? Did the flame really rekindle or has your hope expired and you figure he'll do?

Granted, if enough time has passed and your ex has demonstrated significant growth and maturity—and by that I mean he finally made good on his promise to check into rehab or he underwent six years of psychoanalysis or he attended so many anger-management workshops he developed his own curriculum and now teaches the courses himself at the local community college—then yes, by all means, the potential for a new and improved relationship exists. Very exciting! *You and Your Man 2.0* holds boundless possibilities!

But unless some major changes have occurred, the prognosis for this go-round fares no better than the last six times you took a crack at it. You'll keep forcing the relationship *again*, smashing that square peg into a round hole *again*. And inadvertently, you'll set you both up for some wicked heartache *again*.

Psych 101: Why we do it

Oh, it makes perfect sense. You're so comfortable with him. It feels so familiar. You know exactly what you'd be getting into. In so many ways, going back to your ex provides the perfect solution—a welcome relief from the strain of the single lifestyle. No more anxious first-date jitters. No more boring yourself to tears rattling off your résumé and vital stats to three new guys in one week. You can hit the club and just enjoy your girls, free of the pressure to prowl around the dance floor, keeping one eye peeled for your next boyfriend.

Plus, of all the toads you kissed in your stint back "out there", not one turned into anything remotely regal, though you did manage to meet several court jesters, trolls, and hobbits along the way. After trudging through this ogre-laden Enchanted Forest, your ex starts looking better and better. Maybe you were wrong to let him go. What was all the fuss about, anyway? You probably blew things way out of proportion. Sure he was possessive, controlling, petty, irrational, insensitive, uncouth, and obstinate—but in the most charming way. And hey, maybe he is kind of a jerk, but he's *your* jerk.

Such agile arguments and cogent justifications often serve as sufficient ammunition to usher us back into the arms of an ex. No judgment here. It's completely understandable. Enduring months (or years) of first-date disappointment saps our energy and dampens our spirits. We get really darn tired.

Then the doubts set in. Maybe what we had was as good as it gets. We keep seeking a better match, anticipating an upgrade to a snazzier model, but what if we've been driving the top of the line all along? Our dreams of a superior relationship might be just that—dreams.

Ultimately, this final rationale may prove the most persuasive of all. Not that we would ever *intend* to settle, but after a prolonged stint of being single we begin to lose faith. We convince ourselves that fairy tales don't come true, and we might as well find someone we can be reasonably happy with and call it quits. And though he came with plenty of foibles, your ex made you—well, maybe not quite *happy*, but content. So why not give it another chance?

Furthermore, as we look around and witness the adultery, abuse, and apathy infesting our friends' marriages, we question the logic in waiting for "The One". Even if we meet the perfect boyfriend, won't he, too, eventually morph into the inconsiderate, ungrateful, insensitive creature known as a husband? Is there really such a thing as Mr. Right? Your best friend thought she had him, yet her husband recently confessed to an affair and filed for divorce. A coworker tied the knot last year, but spends every lunch hour badmouthing the man she basically dragged down the aisle. And you certainly can't remember the last time your book club discussed character development or Biblical allusions. No time for such literary discourse—it would cut into the husband-bashing.

We start to think, *If I'm going to be miserable in five years anyway, what's the point of holding out for any particular man? If all guys are about the same, I guess my ex-boyfriend isn't such a bad choice.*

It just hasn't happened yet

I get it, yet I can't support it. And trust me, I've seen it time and time again. Women approach their "scary age" and if no man appears on the horizon, they start flipping through the Rolodex, ready to rustle up a tolerable-enough ex. Memories of arguments and deal-breakers pale in comparison to the thought of showing up solo to Great Aunt Enid's Christmas dinner for the sixth year running.

But I just can't condone returning to the past when the future could be brighter than you can possibly imagine! A wonderful relationship might be coming your way next month, next week, or even tomorrow. To cave and settle for an ex at this point makes no sense whatsoever, especially since you've already made it through the hardest part—the break up and recovery!

Admittedly, some couples have success when giving it another go. And if such a story line lies in your future, more power to you. But if your desire to reconnect with your ex-boyfriend reflects dating scene fatigue and I'll-never-find-a-decent-husband hopelessness, you need a motivational seminar and a shot of caffeine, not a reunification with a former flame.

Sure, marriage is risky business and many husbands stink! They take their wives for granted, grow pot bellies, and amuse themselves in the sack with Dutch Ovens (you know, the thing with the flatulence under the covers. . . ugh!). But for every dud husband, there's a stud husband. And don't you think the chance of a happy marriage increases if you enter the union with someone who excites, thrills, and stimulates you as opposed to someone you dredged up when rummaging through the skeletons in your closet?

Ditto

Dr. Laura Berman, Assistant Clinical Professor of Psychiatry at the Feinberg School of Medicine at Northwestern University, offers the following suggestions for breaking bad ex-boyfriend habits:

"Change your pattern. When relationships get stuck in a revolving rut, it is generally because our lives are stuck in a revolving rut. By changing your routine, you can change your point of view and end a make-up and break-up cycle. . . It might be helpful to keep two lists on hand with you at all times—one list to remind you why the relationship can't work (he doesn't want kids, you don't share similar life goals, etc.), and one list to remind you why you are content and complete as you are (you love the freedom to meet new people, you have a wonderful network of friends and family, etc.)."

Girl Talk

Karin,

Don't you think you're making a really big deal out of nothing? What's your beef with the whole getting back with your ex-boyfriend thing? And by the way, for someone who's usually so positive, you're being really negative here. I mean, you act like people can never get it right once there's been a break-up in their history. Everyone knows that sometimes it takes a while for a couple to work out the kinks. Why would you insist they shouldn't give it a try when this time it might finally work out for them?

So let me take a stab at a little Psych 101 myself. Is this possibly your issue? Were you so horribly traumatized after going around and around with an ex-boyfriend that now you make these big generalizations about the futility of it all? If that's the case, I feel bad for you, of course, but it's not fair to assume that no other couple will be able to get it together just because you guys couldn't.

Besides, look at all the on-again/off-again couples that ended up happily ever after—Bo & Hope, Rachel & Ross, and even Carrie & Big! See, there's hope for all of us!

— Tiffany, 25

Tiff,

Okay, sure, this topic could be considered my issue. I've certainly never managed a clean break with a guy. Every romantic relationship I've ever had has meandered around in the gray area between together and broken up for *at least* several months after the initial split. And the times I've officially reunited with an ex haven't felt so good (despite what the Peaches and Herb song says) and never worked out (obviously—because I'm still single). You might be onto something, though. Maybe I'm coming down a little hard on this because I've never gotten it right myself. Good analysis. Were you a psych major, too?

That being said, I still stand by the points I made in the chapter—especially the idea of holding out for a better fit rather than settling for an ex just because you're so dang weary of dating. Of course you're tired. But you're going to be much more tired trapped in an uninspiring marriage!

As for your TV couples. . . I cheer on my television romances as much as the next girl. But I doubt they represent an argument for getting back with an ex. Remember, those plots are designed to increase Nielsen ratings; they're not meant to serve as "How To" manuals for relationships. Personally, I like watching that kind of drama, but I don't wanna be living it!

— Karin

P.S. Oh, and if you're gonna rattle off famous on-again/off-again TV couples, you need to include Sam & Diane, Ally & Billy, and Felicity & Noel. And none of them made it in the end.

The Awful Truth

Remember, these scenes are not *based* on real stories. They *are* real stories!

ONE MORE TIME, WITH FEELING

CAST.
CASSIE: 29-years-old, recently engaged to
 her on-again/off-again
 boyfriend of 5 years, Rod, a

> high school math teacher and
> soccer coach

LORRAINE: Cassie's best friend and
roommate

INTERIOR -- THE WOMEN'S APARTMENT -
DAY

Cassie and Lorraine are in the middle of a
heated argument.

> LORRAINE
> There's NO WAY you're
> getting married to Rod.
> This is completely absurd,
> Cassie! You guys have
> been in this back-and-
> forth relationship for
> years! And now you've
> been back "on" for 10
> minutes and you're
> engaged? Do you see how
> nutty that is?

CASSIE

This is *so* not what I need
from you right now,
Lorraine. As my best
friend, you should be
happy for me. I always
support you in your
relationships!

LORRAINE

Because I don't date jerks,
Cassie! You have good
reason to support me and
I have good reason to NOT
support you! You've said
yourself that Rod doesn't
treat you right!

CASSIE

But I still keep going back
to him, don't I?

LORRAINE

Because you're crazy.

CASSIE

Because I love him,
Lorraine. And yeah,
we've had our problems
and yeah, we fight. But
at some point in your life
you realize maybe it's not
so much about finding
someone you can live
with, but finding someone
you can't live without.

Lorraine shakes her head, unconvinced.

LORRAINE

Or maybe it's just you're
29 and you're terrified of
being single at 30.

Fast-forward five years:
Cassie and Rod are divorced. Cassie is
raising their daughter alone because Rod
ran off with a high school senior.

Lesson learned: Admittedly, this is an extreme example and the vast majority of our on-again/off-again boyfriends aren't latent pedophiles. Still, it's a good reminder that if you and your man keep breaking up, your relationship is, well, broken. You may not even be able to put your finger on why, but maybe you should trust the natural course of events—you quite possibly may have dodged a bullet. Just walk away.

Guy Talk

So here's where I'm gonna completely disagree with Karin because—well, she's wrong. And I'm not trying to tick her off or anything because she's the one paying me (and by that I mean she's buying me a lot of beer) and I'm sure that when she asked me to provide a guy's perspective, she didn't expect me to challenge her every assertion. But here goes. . .

First of all, I'm a little surprised with her take on this subject because she's doing that infuriating thing so many women do—talking about guys as if we're all the same—and saying that in all cases and at all times, it's a bad idea to get back with an ex-boyfriend because if it didn't work out the first time, it'll never work out during round two. She's basically assuming all guys are fools and none of us should ever be given a second chance. Is she kidding? That just doesn't make sense.

I mean, how can she possibly advise you to never ever go back with an ex? She doesn't know the 411 on your relationships. Besides, timing is everything! I know plenty of couples who split up for a while—he needed time to find himself via a backpacking trip through Europe, or she couldn't see the relationship clearly till she signed up for a clairvoyance certification program in Sedona—but once these individual pursuits were resolved, they came back together and ended up really happy.

That's not to say that some guys don't intentionally use lame reasons to take a sabbatical from a relationship and then saunter on back when they're a) lonely, b) bored, or c) lookin' for some lovin'.

They might serve up all sorts of lines—"I'm commitment phobic," or "I've got to get some stuff out of my system," or "I need to do this on my own, baby." And yeah, in some cases it's complete B.S. But there are also some really nice guys out there who do, in fact, have some instability or immaturity going on and mean it when they give those sorts of explanations. Did you ever think about that, Karin?

Besides, this whole book is a statement against the generalities and assumptions people make about single women, yet you're doing the exact same thing about single men, assuming that they're all trying to win you back just to hurt you again.

And another point Karin fails to make— women do this, too. For example, I have this one friend who left her boyfriend to get back with an ex and then left the ex to get back with the other ex, who she eventually married. Okay, that was really confusing, but the point is, she had to jump in the ring for another round with both ex-boyfriends before her decision became clear. What would Karin have to say about that, huh? (Um, Guy, I know Maria, too. I'm aware of her story. And what I have to say about it is—) **It's not your turn, Karin..** (But you asked!) **It was rhetorical, and you know it!** (Okay, okay, my bad. Carry on. — Karin)

My point is, maybe it wasn't pretty, but Maria needed to go through that mess in order to figure it all out. And it's unfortunate that the bachelors got jerked around and that one came up empty handed but hey, what's the expression? All's fair in love and war...

— Guy

Wow! He had a lot to say about that one, didn't he? I can't figure out if he made a decent argument or if he was just trying to make us feel sorry for all his emotionally unstable friends so we'd go out with them again...

Maybe we're not even disagreeing so much here. Really, it's more about *why* you're getting back with your ex. If you've given up and you're settling, then I stand my ground, but if you've both grown and changed and you've still got the hots for each other, then who am I to stand in your way? Ultimately, this is a complex issue and, hey,

217

now you've got two perspectives to consider and you can decide for yourself. You're a big girl after all.

— Karin

Shout Out!

So to my smart, sexy, cream-of-the-crop, A-list, single friends I say this: You aren't screwed up, you don't need another self-help book, and trying to make a broken relationship work for the hundredth time keeps you focused on the past, missing out on your exciting future. You're great women and you didn't mess up anything with your ex. It just wasn't meant to be. There's nothing more you should or could be doing and nothing you need to change. You can't teach an old relationship new tricks. It just hasn't happened yet.

chapter 11

It Just Hasn't Happened Yet so Take It From Those Who've Been There!

we've got proof!

When I was single I was completely convinced my "intimacy issues" were just too huge and insurmountable and that I would have to be happy with my girlfriends and family and resign myself to never having a romantic relationship. Then I met David and we hit it off easily and immediately and I realized I'd been selling myself short. As for those emotional issues I'd been so worried about? Funny how they magically disappeared once I met the right guy! I'm a good wife and loving partner and I definitely have all the intimacy skills I need to be in a strong marriage.

— Felicia, 45

I know some of you don't believe me. You'd like to, really you would, but you don't. How can we possibly be okay just the way we are? It doesn't make sense. All the normal people we know are happily coupled up and we're not, so something *must* be wrong.

But despite your doubts, you're hanging in—giving me a chance to convince you. Occasionally you truly resonate with a theme, get caught up in the hype, and maybe even blurt out an audible "That's right!" or "You know it!" In those moments you feel totally supported and understood. You embrace the clear and obvious logic of "It just hasn't happened yet" and wonder why no one has ever pulled back the curtain on this issue before. It's time we let single women off the hook!

But then the backlash—that familiar defeatist thinking rears its head, scourging you with doubts and flat-out rejection of my premise. *What does she know anyway? She's still single, isn't she? Please, it's the blind leading the blind! All this book does is tick off items on a single*

woman's Wish List. We wish we were okay 'as is'.
We wish there wasn't anything wrong with us.
We wish it just hadn't happened yet. But come on,
who are we kidding? Sometimes people truly
sabotage their love lives or can't even get into
decent relationships in the first place because
they're blocked by fears of intimacy or they have
trust issues or some other sort of screwed up
condition. You're a psychologist, Karin! You
should know that!

I hear you and I get it. I do. I know it's
hard to fight the onslaught of negative messages
we assimilated long ago from sources we perceived
as trustworthy and reliable. And sure, I
understand the power of dysfunction and
neurosis. In fact, some might find it rather
surprising that a psychologist would take a stance
of "You're fine the way you are." After all, I've
been trained to do the exact opposite—to diagnose
maladaptive cognitions and problematic behavior.

But I won't do it here. I refuse to label
women as pathological based solely on the
criterion of their marital status. And I certainly

won't construct formulaic treatment plans guaranteed to bring about everlasting love and happiness. Such an approach might work for depression or obsessive-compulsive disorder. But in the case of single women and their love lives, it's completely illogical.

PSYCH 101: WHY WE DO IT

We challenge the "It just hasn't happened yet" message because it's a new concept for us and old habits—in this case, habitual ways of thinking—die hard. Adjusting our cognitive-default settings requires an enormous amount of effort. And some of us just can't let go of the idea that we need to change something about ourselves before we'll be ready for Mr. Right. As we've already discussed, it's a control thing. I understand.

That being said, I'm not trying to assert that single women should slack off and abandon any efforts toward self-improvement. Not in the least! If you're unhappy with an aspect of your life, by all means, address it. Irritated by some annoying tendency or trait? Fix it! Got issues? Work through them! Looking for insight into who you are? See a therapist! I'm all for self-exploration and edification. Take a meditation class, visit an ashram, hire a life coach, or reconnect with the religious upbringing of your youth. Become whoever it is you're meant to become. But please don't expect some sort of karmic exchange, *à la I cleaned up my act and addressed* [insert pet pathology here] *so I've done my part. Now my man is sure to show up!*

It just hasn't happened yet

Still don't believe me? Can't get on board with the idea that you're fine just the way you are? Let me put it another way.

Self-help reasoning (or that of anyone else who's weighing in) assumes single women possess pesky imperfections and eccentricities which prevent us from snagging a man. So by this line of thinking, such personality shortcomings would appear much less frequently in the population of happily married women, right? Doubtful. Ask any husband—he'll tell you. Wives show a full range of behaviors, quirks, and idiosyncrasies, just like the rest of us. After all, they may be wives, but they're still human.

Even better, many of our happily married friends exhibit extreme versions of the very traits that supposedly stymie our success. Often, in fact, these characteristics constitute key elements in their marital dynamics. Observe any couple. It doesn't take a degree in psychology to note the complementary nature of compatibility. Nutty women find husbands who like drama queens. Needy women secure men who enjoy being needed. If the match occurs at the expected time in a woman's life (typically in her mid-to-late 20s) everyone smiles, applauds, and buys a place setting off her gift registry. No one cares that the bride's a little loopy or that she lacks even a shred of self-reliance. No one mentions the neuroses cementing the marital union. No one frets about Little Miss Nutty or Little Miss Needy because they've become Little *Mrs.* Nutty and Little *Mrs.* Needy.

But a single woman with the exact same instability issues as Little Mrs. Nutty or the dependency issues of Little Mrs. Needy is suspect. With the best intentions, others tell her she better do some soul searching to figure out what's wrong—what's keeping her single. Is this a fair analysis? Or more importantly, is it even remotely accurate? Hardly! Yet, every day single women yield to this nonsense, feeling cruddy and inferior.

Ditto

In preparing for this chapter, I interviewed women who'd been there—women who remained single longer than they'd expected, women who'd endured periods of self-doubt along the way, acknowledging that, at times, they'd wondered what the problem was, why love seemed so hard to find. Each woman stated emphatically that she wished she'd known then what she knows now—that there was *nothing* wrong with her whatsoever—it just hadn't happened yet. I asked them to provide some words of wisdom in the form of a quote that had inspired them during their single years. Here are some of my favorites:

"It's a funny thing about life: if you refuse to accept anything but the very best, you will very often get it."   — W. Somerset Maugham

"Don't compromise yourself. You are all you've got."   — Janis Joplin

"Living in the moment means letting go of the past and not waiting for the future. It means living your life consciously, aware that each moment you breathe is a gift."   — Oprah Winfrey

"Real life isn't always going to be perfect or go our way, but the recurring acknowledgement of what is working in our lives can help us not only survive but surmount our difficulties."

— Sarah Ban Breathnach

"I've learned from experience that the greater part of our happiness or misery depends on our dispositions and not on our circumstances."

— Martha Washington

"We must be willing to get rid of the life we've planned, so as to have the life that is waiting for us."

— Joseph Campbell

Girl Talk

Karin,

Let me take a moment to weigh in as "one who's been there". As a single woman living in New York during my 20s and 30s, I heard every explanation in the proverbial book (and those from your book, as a matter of fact) as to why I was unattached.

Did I get tired of all the unsolicited advice and lame prescriptions to treat my "problem"? Definitely! And of course people told me I was "too picky" but I was okay with that because I refused to consider spending my life with someone who didn't really fit the bill. So I waited for the right one, but he took his time showing up, and I didn't get married until I was 43.

Personally, I think that smart and accomplished women have it harder because many men seem to want to dominate. But that's all the more reason to wait for the right one, a guy who can really appreciate your intelligence and accomplishments. You want a partner, after all, not a daddy or a kid to care for.

But for me, because it took so long to find the right guy, I had to give up my desire to have children. That's a very real sacrifice. I did try to get pregnant on my own in my late 30s via a sperm bank, and when that didn't work and I was faced with considering more invasive procedures, I had to do some real soul-searching. Finally I decided that I would rather have a good partner than a child by myself (because it would probably become even harder to find someone if I were a

*parent). But that is in the mix there, too. And I think
when we get to a certain age, women may have to make
that choice.*

— *Erin, 45*

Erin,

Hmmm. So I intended this chapter to
substantiate my point with the testimonies of
women who withstood the pressure to settle and
ended up happily married, even if it took longer
than they expected. But you bring up a very real
concern and one that I haven't touched on.

And maybe I haven't dealt with it because
it's a sad, not-so-encouraging reality of the single
woman's journey. By waiting for the right guy we
may miss out on the chance to have it all. Like you
said, some of us might have to make a choice at
some point. Do we freeze our eggs, hoping Mr.
Right will eventually show? Or find a sperm
donor and try to get pregnant solo? Should we
marry the okay guy we're dating because he'll
make a good father?

It's hard to talk about because it stinks to think that a woman who did the right thing by waiting for the right husband, a woman who is emotionally stable and economically secure and who wants to be a mother, wouldn't get the chance. Unfortunately, your experience clearly shows that sometimes that's what happens. It's tough and unfair and I'm sorry.

— Karin

The Awful Truth

Remember, these scenes are not *based* on real stories. They *are* real stories!

LOVE ENOUGH FOR BOTH?

CAST.
JANE: 32-year-old grad student, engaged to be married

VANESSA: 35-year-old grad student and
Jane's classmate

INTERIOR -- CONDOMINIUM IN THE CITY -
DAY

Jane and Vanessa are in the midst of an
intense discussion. Jane has been crying
and is trying to compose herself.

> JANE
> It's not that I don't love
> my fiancé, Vanessa. I *do*.
> It's just that it doesn't
> feel quite right. But what
> does *right* feel like,
> anyway?

> VANESSA
> This may be hard to hear,
> Jane, but I can tell you I
> had similar misgivings
> before I married my first
> husband.

JANE

I didn't know you were
married before.

VANESSA

Oh, yeah. I had a starter
marriage a few years ago.

JANE

Really? What happened?

VANESSA

Well, he was perfect—at
least on paper. Derek
had a great job, lots of
money, owned a couple
homes—the whole nine
yards. And I had just
turned 30 and my
parents were pressuring
me and everyone was
like, "What's the matter?
Why aren't you married
yet?" You know, the
typical stuff single women

hear. Plus, I was really
anxious to have children
and was scared that time
was running out. So I
guess in a way I gave in
to their expectations and
my fear of never
becoming a mom.

JANE
What happened?

VANESSA
Well, we got engaged and
I was a complete wreck
the entire time—horrible
jitters and cold feet. I
literally was dreading the
wedding, but went
through with it anyway
because, you know, I'd
waited long enough for
"Mr. Right" so "Mr.
Pretty Close and Loaded"
would have to do. Plus he

was crazy about me. I
guess I figured he loved
me enough for both of us.

JANE

But it didn't last, huh?

VANESSA

Nope. His love was
enough for both of us
until I met a struggling
documentary filmmaker
who made my heart do
back flips. How's that old
song go? "It's sad to
belong to someone else
when the right one comes
along." Well it is. And it
was.

Lesson learned: Let's skip the starter marriages and
early divorces. How 'bout we spend our man-free
time enjoying who we are and learning about who

we're becoming? Take it from those who've been there—it's best to wait for the right one.

Guy Talk

It's that Biological Clock thing again, isn't it? Of course guys can never quite understand it. How could we? Our little swimmers stay strong into our 60s and 70s so fatherhood is something we can wait on.

Now as for this "choice thing" Erin's talking about—Karin addressed it a little in the "Too Picky" chapter and I didn't weigh in on it then, but I'm going to now.

Hear me loud and clear, ladies. Just wait for the right guy already! I mean, freeze your eggs if you want to or find yourself a sperm donor; I don't have a problem with any of that. But the one option I'd ask you <u>not</u> to consider is settling for some dude just because you think he'd be a good father. Because that's not really fair to the guy now is it?

This really hit me a while ago with a woman I was dating. She was smart, funny, successful, beautiful, had a great group of friends, and a very full life. She also happened to be a few years older than I and had just turned 39. She was incredibly energetic and upbeat about life in general, but every once in a while she'd get real down. And when I'd ask her what was wrong, she'd be like, "I don't have a baby and the chances of me ever having one are getting slimmer and slimmer and it's depressing." Of course I tried to listen and be sensitive, and I'd remind her that she'd made a lot of choices in her life that had brought her to this place. Um, apparently that was the WRONG thing to say because she'd go through the roof! She said I had no clue what the motherhood meant to a woman and you know what? I think she was right.

We ended up breaking up after a few months and I don't think it was because of that, but I do have to say that although we weren't very compatible, I felt like she might have kept on with me because I represented maybe her last chance to have a kid. And that didn't sit well with me at all.

So, like I said, don't do that to your boyfriend. Guys want to be loved for themselves, not for their sperm.

— Guy

Guy,

Let me get this out of the way first: If telling a 39-year-old woman that it's her fault she's single and childless is your idea of being sensitive, we really need to have a heart-to-heart! I know you, so I understand you were trying to be supportive, but, trust me, all you did was make her feel way worse.

And clearly you get it—that there's no way you can completely understand what being a mother means to a woman. Motherhood and fatherhood are vastly different constructs in our culture (and probably in most other cultures, too). You can't really imagine how much pressure we feel to procreate. We're hit with the "mommy mandate" early and often. While little boys play with trucks and beat each other up at recess, we feed our baby dolls, put them down for naps, and change their diapers. The vast majority of us never considered the possibility of *not* being mothers someday. And even if we love our careers and adore our friends and think we have utterly fantastic lives, most of us will have to grieve the loss of not having children if that is, in fact, the hand we're dealt.

I suppose we got off topic a bit, but Erin brought it up and I didn't want to ignore the subject. That's not fair to do when it's a reality some of us will face.

— Karin

Shout Out!

So to my smart, sexy, cream-of-the-crop, A-list, single friends I say this: You aren't screwed up, you don't need another self-help book, and millions of women can attest to the fact that it'll happen eventually. You're great women and you didn't mess anything up; don't *create* a mess by rushing into something because you've given up hope. There's nothing more you should or could be doing and nothing you need to change. Keep the faith! It just hasn't happened yet.

chapter 12

It Just Hasn't Happened Yet so Get on with Your Fabulous Life!

you're no "Lady in Waiting"

My friends are always giving me the "Your time will come" line. As if I'm just stuck in some dead-end waiting room, holding a ticket, hoping that any moment my number will be called and then my life can suddenly begin and I'll be happy! It makes me want to rip out my hair every time. . . and then, how am I gonna get a guy without any hair?

— Corrine, 27

So sneaky, so subtle, so surreptitious. We don't even know we're doing it, but we are. Even if we do become aware of it, we still probably think it's okay. Unless someone challenges us on it, we see no need to change. But it keeps us miserable, detached, and, arguably, half alive.

When I get a boyfriend. . . When I get engaged. . . When it's my wedding. . . When I get pregnant. . . When I have a family. . . When! When! When! Living for *when*—what a waste of a life!

And yet so many single women adopt this "Lady in Waiting" stance. We put our lives on hold until the *whens* occur. Nothing we do matters all that much until we can check these objectives off the list. Until then, we float in limbo. Sure we look like we're living, but we're not. We're *waiting*.

"Ladies in Waiting" fall along various points on a wide continuum. In some cases, a woman postpones normal, age-appropriate life decisions and completely avoids participating in certain events. She eats off paper plates in lieu of purchasing dinnerware since she'll eventually end up registering for everything once she's engaged and what if her future husband wants to weigh in on the flatware and stemware selections? Others put off vacation plans. Who wants to go to Paris with girlfriends? Everyone knows it's a city for lovers. This "Lady in Waiting" maintains she'd rather wait and save the trip for her honeymoon.

A more flagrant, yet unfortunately not uncommon, variation of the "Lady in Waiting" mindset causes a woman to essentially live the life she *expects* to have one day, while thoroughly minimizing and dismissing the life she *actually lives*. She's the gal with more baby toys in her apartment than furniture. In preparation for motherhood, she's been stocking up on items from *Pottery Barn Kids* and *Janie and Jack* for years. At 30, she still furnishes her living room with cinder block book shelves but has shelled out $15,000 to outfit a second bedroom into the most charming nursery! Granted, she has neither husband nor baby in sight, but that's just a slight technicality.

But by far the most debilitating and insidious infestation of the "Lady in Waiting" mentality plagues most of us most of the time in an ongoing mental commentary. Overtly, we live our lives—make adult purchases and take grown-up vacations—but a continuous clandestine commentary exposes our true attitudes:

- On our way to buy dinnerware: *This would be so much more fun if I were picking out china patterns with my fiancé and not stuck doing this all alone.*

- With our friends at a café on the Champs-Élysées: *Paris! The City of Lights! How romantic! Everything would be perfect if this were a getaway with my gorgeous husband. Too bad I'm just here with the girls.*

- Strolling through the mall: *I know it would be stupid to buy this Vera Bradley diaper bag now, but I really wish I were in the market for one. When will I get my chance to be a mom? [sigh]*

Psych 101: Why we do it

It's simple, really. With the placing of a pink crocheted bonnet on our newborn heads, the programming and conditioning commenced. As little girls, every fairy tale we heard began with *Once upon a time* and ended with *happily ever after*—and not once did *happily ever after* occur without a prince. In adolescence, *Seventeen* magazine convinced us that our "Dream Prom" necessitated a "Dream Date"—anything less would leave us less than happy; going stag or with girlfriends was clearly second best. And college merely upped the ante. Firmly indoctrinated in our women's studies, we gave lip service to existentialist feminism and consciousness-raising, but that didn't assuage our angst that Homecoming loomed in the near future and we had yet to secure a date.

Throughout our formative years, in countless ways, our culture bombarded us with the message, "Your happiness won't be complete until you meet your man." And before we had the wherewithal to question or protest, we'd internalized this rigid philosophy, becoming bona fide "Ladies in Waiting".

It just hasn't happened yet

Okay, fine. We may have unwittingly inherited this philosophy, but we're older and wiser now. We know better. It's high time we protested this pitiful perspective. Assuming a "Lady in Waiting" stance is no way to live!

Every adage applies: "You only go around once in life." "This isn't a dress rehearsal." "All we have is the present moment." Clichés or not, they're true! My 8th grade English teacher used to say, "Time is life and life is time. If you waste time, you're committing suicide." She had a point—one that many single women should take to heart. If we embrace a "Lady in Waiting" mentality, we commit a slow form of suicide.

Perhaps that seems a tad drastic, but think about your stance on life and time. Do we savor every phase, enjoying all the wonderful things happening *right now*? Or do we wish our lives away, judging our own existence as inferior until a man materializes to legitimize us? Do we create full and exciting lives, utilizing the breadth of our gifts, talents, and abilities? Or do we passively squander precious hours, days, and months waiting for the *whens*? Do we relish our amazing friendships and family connections, or do we minimize these relationships, refusing to be happy with just about anything in our lives until we snag a husband?

Waiting, waiting, waiting, for "The One". But what if he never shows up? What does that make—a worthless life? If you consent to the "Lady in Waiting" philosophy, that's essentially what you're asserting. Are you prepared to say that about yourself and your single girlfriends? Why would you want to?

It's a choice. Simple as that. A choice. You can choose to plod through every day, crossing it off on your calendar, thankful only to make it one step closer to the day you find your man. Or you can approach life as an adventure you create for yourself—on your terms and according to your ideology and standards. It's up to you.

If you're ready to chuck the "Lady in Waiting" mentality, here are a few tenets to try on for size:

- So I'm single. So what? It's not my fault or anything. It just hasn't happened yet.

- My mother lived her life and I'm living mine. Of course she harbors some hopes and dreams for me, but I'm not about to cave to any pressure she may throw my way just to guarantee her a couple grandkids.

- Yeah, maybe I am picky and I intend to stay that way!

- Listen, I'm as "out there" as I'm ever gonna get so deal with it!

- Tone it down? What a ridiculous concept! It would never even occur to me to be anything less than my fabulous self.

- When it comes to love, trying or not trying is hardly the issue. I'm living my life my way and I won't feel obligated to appease others' expectations of how I manage my pursuit of relationships.

- I have many fascinating and intriguing things to think about each day. I won't waste good neural energy obsessing about men.

- Everyone travels a unique journey in life. I don't need to compare myself to my friends. Where they are right now is great for them; where I am right now is great for me. I'm not worried about keeping up with Joan or Lily or Kaitlyn.

- If I want to do some online dating, I will. But I won't allow myself to feel obligated.

- I expect a future full of boyfriends who will blow my ex-boyfriends out of the water. No time for regressing into the ex-fray.

- When frustrated, I'll look to the women who've been there—who have heard all the nonsense I hear, but who stuck to their guns and waited for the right guy.

- I value my life and myself for who I am—not who I'm with. I'm living to the fullest now!

And of course, if a wonderful man shows up and you decide to let him come along for the ride, fantastic. Lucky him! And then, just like that, it will have happened.

Ditto

The title of Peggy Orenstein's book, *Flux: Women on Sex, Work, Kids, Love, and Life in a Half-Changed World*, says it all. Today we revel in revenues reaped from the relentless efforts of countless women over the last hundred years. We thank our mothers and grandmothers for paving the way, leaving a legacy of unprecedented prerogatives for our self definition. But it's still a half changed world in which we live and, as Orenstein asserts, we women are partly responsible:

"If women can't see single life as a viable alternative with its own set of costs, rewards, and challenges, then they remain as controlled by marriage as previous generations, equally vulnerable to making choices negatively—out of fear instead of authentic desire."

Girl Talk

Dear Karin,

Yeah, yeah, yeah. I know you're right, and I get that it's lame to be a "Lady in Waiting" and all, but you make it sound so easy and it's NOT! I mean, come on! It is more fun to pick out plates if someone other than you is going to eat off them and it is way better to be in the most romantic city in the world with a guy than with the girls and it is tempting to buy diaper bags even when you're single—especially if they're Vera Bradley! Plus, this year has been the worst because I've been in—count 'em—four weddings and it's tough not dreaming about my own wedding while helping my girls with theirs. Is that so wrong? So what if I've already bought my wedding planner, picked out my color palette, selected my bridal party and chosen the song my husband and I will dance to during the reception. I'm just getting caught up in the hype. And no, I don't have a boyfriend right now, but I want to be prepared for when that day comes!

— Missy, 27

Dear Missy,

You've got the living in the "whens" thing down pat, don't you? With your "have wedding, insert groom" mentality, you'll be more than ready when that day comes—which, admittedly, will be quite efficient because you'll already have finished a lot of the wedding prep so you'll be able to really enjoy your engagement and not be so stressed out.

But at the same time, have you thought about how your groom will feel knowing you picked out a song representing your undying love for each other when you didn't even know who the heck he was? Seems a bit odd to me, but, hey, I'm not trying to spoil your fun or anything.

And if it is, in fact, fun for you, then tell me to shut-up and I'll back off, but I can't help but wonder why you're giving all this time in your 20s—time that should be all about *you*, enjoying *you*, discovering *you*—to some man you've never met and to a love you haven't experienced yet.

I'm wondering if it's a case of no one validating your life and your choices right now, so you don't either. Maybe with all your girls getting married, there's no room to appreciate anything other than matrimonial "accomplishments". Everything else is just a consolation prize. I think I can relate.

In my late 20s, I began pursuing my doctorate in psychology. Now—I'm definitely a bit sensitive (and perhaps somewhat paranoid), but I remember feeling that when people learned what I was doing they were interested and impressed— which was great, of course—but I also sensed that at least of some of them questioned whether I'd be working on a graduate degree if my personal life were in a different place. Almost a *well, it's nice she's filling up her time with school since she doesn't have a husband and children. . .*

Again, my thin skin may have bruised a bit too easily, but my point is, I know how it feels when friends unintentionally devalue your life. And you might be constructing your TBA-wedding with your TBA-groom in efforts to stay in the loop with your friends—to be where they are and a part of their scene—because that's what matters to them. But in the end, you're just disparaging your life, your circumstances, and ultimately, yourself.

— Karin

The Awful Truth

Remember, these scenes are not *based* on real stories. They *are* real stories!

YOU CAN'T RUSH A GOOD THING

CAST.
TAMMY: 21-year-old, college junior
KRISTIN: Tammy's best friend and
            roommate

INTERIOR -- COLLEGE DORM ROOM - DAY

Kristin is headed to class and has
accidentally grabbed some of Tammy's
notebooks. She's flipping through them
when Tammy walks in.

                    KRISTIN
          You've got some
          explaining to do,
          girlfriend.

                    TAMMY
          What are you talking
          about?

KRISTIN

I'm not sure, but let's see
if we can make sense of
it. You and Paul started
dating, what—two weeks
ago? And now you've
devoted an entire page of
your Sociology notebook
to sketching out your
wedding party and
writing variations of your
new name—"Tammy
Bates Hutchinson" and
"Mr. and Mrs. Paul
Hutchinson"—seriously?

TAMMY

So what?

KRISTIN

So what? That's totally
lame! That's what!

TAMMY

I know, I know. I'm
supposed to be all Ms.
Independent and stuff,
but I can't help it. I get
excited about being
married someday. And
honestly, I just don't feel
complete without a guy.
I'm not the only one, you
know. Women are made
that way, Kristin!

KRISTIN

Hey, there's nothing
wrong with wanting to get
married someday, but
may I remind you that
you're only 21 years old
and you've been dating
Paul for all of two weeks?
And may I also remind
you that a few years ago
there was this thing
called Women's Liberation

and women of our
generation are supposed
to be the beneficiaries of
the changes this
movement brought about.

TAMMY
Huh? You lost me.

KRISTIN
No kidding! Maybe if you
paid a little more
attention in Sociology, you
might know what I'm
talking about.

Kristin pauses and shakes her head.

KRISTIN
But, hey, thanks for the
maid-of-honor nod.
Should I get fitted for my
gown right away or wait
another two weeks till
you're officially engaged?

Lesson Learned: Some "Ladies in Waiting" won't respond to interventions. Refusing to acknowledge their worth *sans* husbands, they hold out on life while holding out for Mr. Right. Our fabulousness is a choice, you know. We decide it, create it, and live it. Or we don't. But *we* determine our value and *we* ascribe meaning to who we are and what we're about.

Guy Talk

This is another one that's hard for me to get. And it's probably because of all the stuff Karin keeps harping on—how men and women are socialized differently and that a man's worth is determined by his career and income, but women remain judged by the man they're with. And even as I write that I think, "Really? Still? That's so lame!" But I've read this whole book, too, and I guess Karin convinced me along the way. (Woo hoo! We got through to him! — Karin)

That being said, I certainly hope things begin to change. Maybe this generation of men can help improve things for the future. I mean, I think about being a father someday and how I'll instill everything I can into my daughter. And of course she'll be talented, intelligent, ambitious, and charismatic and I'll adore her and tell her how wonderful she is. So I'd hate to think that somehow she wouldn't really believe herself to be all these things unless she was dating some dude. I mean, what about the father who loves and adores her? My opinion doesn't matter? The only thing that makes her feel worthwhile is if she's arm-and-arm with some guy with a slick suit, gelled-up hair, and impressive résumé? I am <u>not</u> okay with that! She could end up rushing into marrying some bonehead just to keep up with the Joans and earn society's blessing but then be miserable for the rest of her life! Have you thought about <u>that</u>? This has got to stop!

— Guy

Well yes, Guy, we have thought about that. It's basically what I've been talking about for the last 250 or so pages. But that was really sweet. You're not even a father yet and you're already championing your daughter's value and worth. Awesome!

— Karin

Shout Out!

So to my smart, sexy, cream-of-the-crop, A-list, single friends I say this: You aren't screwed up, you don't need another self-help book, and you've got a fabulous life going on—if only you'll grab onto it! There's nothing more you should or could be doing and nothing you need to change. No "Ladies in Waiting" here. It just hasn't happened yet!

Afterword

Thanks for picking up the book and giving it a read. I hope you've found yourself encouraged, emboldened, and empowered! Ideally, the next time someone says something insensitive (or flat out stupid) about you being single, you'll think back to the themes we've discussed here and laugh it off with a, "Whatever! It just hasn't happened yet!"

If you want to join the conversation, check out my website AuthenticallyMe.com, a forum for women exploring ways to maintain their identities in the midst (or in spite) of their most intimate relationships.

On the site there's a page devoted to *It Just Hasn't Happened Yet* where you'll find complimentary bonus features: a downloadable *It Just Hasn't Happened Yet* journal for reflection, reinforcement of all the topics covered in the book, and additional Girl Talks just for *you*!

AUTHENTICALLY ✿ ME

Acknowledgments

I am deeply and forever indebted to my parents, Dr. Simon and Nancy Anderson, who, by their example, taught me to live each day to its fullest, dream big dreams, and find, no matter what life throws at me, a way to "get happy". Thanks to my brothers, Warren, for frequent and skillful editing, and Elliott, who inspired me to "make it happen" by writing his own book.

Much gratitude to my team at Clifton Hills Press—Colleen McSwiggin, for believing in my message and bringing a keen mind and sharp focus to this project, and Erin O'Connor, for ingenuity, tenacity, and charm—may this be the beginning of a long, rewarding partnership.

Finally, thanks to the many single women who graciously shared their stories with me. Your candor gave this book its voice.

References

"**Ditto**" Sections:

Chapter 1:
De Paulo, B. (2006). *Singled out: How singles are stereotyped, stigmatized, and ignored and still live happily ever after.* New York: St. Martin's Press.

Chapter 2:
Trimberger, E. K. (2005). *The new single woman.* Boston: Beacon Press.

Chapter 3:
Talbot, L. (2007, Aug. 21). Stop Singlism! *Forbes.com.* Retrieved from http://www.forbes.com/2007/08/21/talbot-singles-discrimination-forbeslife-singles07_cx_lt_0821talbot.html

Chapter 4:

Trimberger, E. K. (2005). *The new single woman.* Boston: Beacon Press.

Chapter 5:

Cochrane, K. (2006). Marriage and terrorism—a dangerous mix. *Guardian.co.uk.* Retrieved from http://www.guardian.co.uk/world/2006/jun/01/gender.lifeandhealth

Harris, L. (2006). Newsweek: OK, singles, now you can worry about terrorism. *Salon.* Retrieved from http://www.salon.com/life/broadsheet/2006/05/24/newsweek_marriage/index.html

DePaulo, B. (2006). *Singled out: How singles are stereotyped, stigmatized, and ignored and still live happily ever after.* New York: St. Martin's Press.

Chapter 6:

Irvine, A. (2009, Nov. 11). Thanks but I don't need you to hook me up. *CNN.com.* Retrieved from

http://www.cnn.com/2009/LIVING/personal/11
/11/rrants.exhibit.a/index.html

Chapter 7:

Lue, N. (2005). Stop obsessing over how men
communicate. *Baggage Reclaim*. Retrieved from
http://www.baggagereclaim.co.uk/stop-
obsessing-over-how-men-communicate/

Chapter 8:

De Paulo, B. (2006). *Singled out: How singles are
stereotyped, stigmatized, and ignored and still live
happily ever after.* New York: St. Martin's Press.

Greenwald, M. (n.d.) Being credentialed.
UnmarriedAmerica.org. Retrieved from
http://www.unmarriedamerica.org/beingcred.ht
ml

Chapter 9:

Reilly, L. (1996). *Women living single: Thirty
women share their stories of navigating through a
married world.* Boston: Faber & Faber.

Chapter 10:

Berman, L. (2008, July 3). Can't quit your ex? How to say goodbye for good: You're better off alone! Don't get stuck in a "make up/break up." *MSNBC.com* Retrieved from http://today.msnbc.msn.com/id/25335116/ns/today-today_relationships/print/1/displaymode/1098/

Chapter 12:

Orenstein, P. (2000). *Flux: Women on sex, work, kids, love, and life in a half-changed world.* New York: Doubleday.

Information about the author

Born in Cincinnati, Ohio, Karin Anderson is currently an associate professor of Psychology and Counselor Education at Concordia University Chicago. She received her doctorate in developmental psychology from Northern Illinois University and has delivered a number of well-received presentations at national and international psychology conferences, covering issues such as identity development and family dynamics.

She first became interested in the psychology of women when she began to examine the complex emotions involved in her own engagement to be married. As she questioned her motivations for marriage, she pondered women's roles and options in the post-feminism era. How much had really changed? After months of internal conflict, she ended up calling off her wedding two months before it was to occur.

Back "out there" in the dating scene, she became keenly aware of the messages directed toward single women—messages that appeared disparaging and illogical, yet hailed from reliable sources such as the local bookstore's self-help section. Drawing on the data of other academic researchers and first hand accounts of the many women she interviewed personally, Anderson wrote *It Just Hasn't Happened Yet* as an effort to provide a logical counter-message of encouragement.

A compelling teacher and speaker, Anderson speaks to groups on women's issues, single adulthood, developmental psychology, and family relationships. For more information, visit AuthenticallyMe.com.

LaVergne, TN USA
22 December 2010
209935LV00001B/61/P